NATIONAL ISSUES
IN
SCIENCE AND TECHNOLOGY
1993

Science and Technology Leadership in American Government:
Ensuring the Best Presidential Appointments

Climate Change Policy:
Establishing United States Leadership Under the
Climate Change Convention

Technology Policy and Industrial Innovation:
The Federal Government's Role

Toward More Effective Health Care Reform:
Selected Issues from Reports of the Institute of Medicine

Summaries of Selected Recent Reports of the
National Research Council

NATIONAL ACADEMY OF SCIENCES
NATIONAL ACADEMY OF ENGINEERING
INSTITUTE OF MEDICINE
NATIONAL RESEARCH COUNCIL

NATIONAL ACADEMY PRESS
Washington, DC 1993

NOTICE: The production of this volume was approved by the Governing Board of the National Research Council, whose members are drawn from the councils of the National Academy of Sciences, the National Academy of Engineering, and the Institute of Medicine.

The material included in the volume is based on the work of duly appointed study committees, the members of which were chosen for their special competencies and with regard for appropriate balance. The white papers and report summaries presented here are drawn from--and faithfully represent--the reports produced by these study committees, which were reviewed by a group other than the authors according to procedures approved by a Report Review Committee consisting of members of the National Academy of Sciences, the National Academy of Engineering, and the Institute of Medicine.

The National Academy of Sciences is a private, nonprofit, self-perpetuating society of distinguished scholars engaged in scientific and engineering research, dedicated to the furtherance of science and technology and to their use for the general welfare. Upon the authority of the charter granted to it by the Congress in 1863, the Academy has a mandate that requires it to advise the federal government on scientific and technical matters. Dr. Frank Press is president of the National Academy of Sciences.

The National Academy of Engineering was established in 1964, under the charter of the National Academy of Sciences, as a parallel organization of outstanding engineers. It is autonomous in its administration and in the selection of its members, sharing with the National Academy of Sciences the responsibility for advising the federal government. The National Academy of Engineering also sponsors engineering programs aimed at meeting national needs, encourages education and research, and recognizes the superior achievements of engineers. Dr. Robert M. White is president of the National Academy of Engineering.

The Institute of Medicine was established in 1970 by the National Academy of Sciences to secure the services of eminent members of appropriate professions in the examination of policy matters pertaining to the health of the public. The Institute acts under the responsibility given to the National Academy of Sciences by its congressional charter to be an adviser to the federal government and, upon its own initiative, to identify issues of medical care, research, and education. Dr. Kenneth I. Shine is president of the Institute of Medicine.

The National Research Council was organized by the National Academy of Sciences in 1916 to associate the broad community of science and technology with the Academy's purposes of furthering knowledge and of advising the federal government. Functioning in accordance with general policies determined by the Academy, the Council has become the principal operating agency of both the National Academy of Sciences and the National Academy of Engineering in providing services to the government, the public, and the scientific and engineering communities. The Council is administered jointly by both Academies and the Institute of Medicine. Dr. Frank Press and Dr. Robert M. White are chairman and vice chairman, respectively, of the National Research Council.

Library of Congress Catalog Card Number 93-83935
International Standard Book Number 0-309-04882-6

Additional copies available from:

National Academy Press
2101 Constitution Avenue, NW
Washington, DC 20418

B-138

Printed in the United States of America

PREFACE

Following the precedent established during the Presidential transition in 1988, the presidents of the National Academy of Sciences (NAS), the National Academy of Engineering (NAE), and the Institute of Medicine (IOM) decided again in 1992 to authorize the preparation of a series of short "white papers" on important national policy issues in which science and technology play a central role. Each paper was drawn from studies undertaken by the Academy complex in recent years. One of the papers--dealing with the problem of recruiting the most outstanding scientific and technical talent for senior Presidential appointments--was conveyed shortly after the election to Warren Christopher and others managing the President-elect's transition effort. The other papers were made available to senior officials of the Clinton administration in the weeks following the Inauguration.

Four white papers are presented: (1) "Science and Technology Leadership in American Government: Ensuring the Best Presidential Appointments"; (2) "Climate Change Policy: Establishing United States Leadership under the Climate Change Convention"; (3) "Technology Policy and Industrial Innovation: The Federal Government's Role"; and (4) "Toward More Effective Health Care Reform". The first three papers are distillations of major reports of blue ribbon panels organized under the auspices of the Academies' Committee on Science, Engineering, and Public Policy (COSEPUP). The fourth paper is a new synthesis of major health policy issues that previously have been addressed by the Institute of Medicine.

The NAS, NAE, and IOM Presidents also authorized the preparation of brief summaries of ten potentially high impact reports issued during the previous 18-24 months by various committees of the National Research Council (NRC), which they jointly manage. The summaries are representative of the more than 200 studies produced annually by the NRC. Copies of the complete NRC reports summarized in this volume, as well as the COSEPUP and IOM reports on which the white papers are based, may be obtained by contacting the National Academy Press (202/334-3313).

Many individuals on or associated with the professional staff of the National Research Council contributed to or commented on the material presented in this volume. The white papers that were based on COSEPUP reports were in each case prepared by the individual who had previously served as director of the study (listed in the same order as above): Michael G.H. McGeary, Robert A. Coppock, and John S. Wilson. Karl D. Yordy, director of the IOM Division of Health Care Services, and Kathleen N. Lohr and Marilyn J. Field, also of the IOM Division of Health Care Services, wrote the IOM white paper. The ten brief summaries of the recent NRC reports were prepared by professional writers Steve Olson and Ethel M. ("Pepper") Leeper and were reviewed extensively by the originating NRC program units. Members of the NRC staff who provided review comments and suggestions were: Stephen R. Godwin, Anne Y. Kester, Mehadevan Mani, Peter B. Myers, Stephen Rattien, Susanne A. Stoiber, Robert E.

Skinner, Miron L. Straf, Paul R. Thomas, Raymond A. Wassel, Arch L. Wood, Suzanne H. Woolsey, and Catherine E. Woteki. Decisions on the selection of NRC reports to be included and quality management of the white papers was undertaken by an editorial commitee consisting of: Lawrence E. McCray, Stephen A. Merrill, Don I. Phillips, and Myron F. Uman. The committee was chaired by Mitchel B. Wallerstein, deputy executive officer of the NRC, who also managed the production of this volume.

CONTENTS

NATIONAL ISSUES
IN
SCIENCE AND TECHNOLOGY
1993

I

SCIENCE AND TECHNOLOGY LEADERSHIP IN AMERICAN GOVERNMENT

Ensuring the Best Presidential Appointments

NATIONAL ACADEMY OF SCIENCES
NATIONAL ACADEMY OF ENGINEERING
INSTITUTE OF MEDICINE

NATIONAL ACADEMY OF SCIENCES
NATIONAL ACADEMY OF ENGINEERING
INSTITUTE OF MEDICINE
2101 Constitution Avenue, Washington, D.C. 20418

January 6, 1993

The Honorable John H. Gibbons
Assistant to the President for Science
  and Technology and Director, Office
  of Science and Technology Policy
Office of Science and Technology Policy
Executive Office of the President
Washington, DC 20506

Dear Jack:

     We congratulate you on your appointment as Assistant to the
President for Science and Technology and Director of the Office
of Science and Technology Policy, and we look forward to working
with you in the coming years. Last month, we submitted to Warren
Christopher, who was then Director of the Presidential Transition
Office, the enclosed summary of our recent report, "Science and
Technology Leadership in American Government: Ensuring the Best
Presidential Appointments," whose principal recommendation was
that the science advisor should be among the earliest of the
President's senior advisors identified and announced, so that he
could make input on the selection of other senior officials
responsible for S&T matters. In this regard, the news of your
early appointment was especially welcome.

     We are sending you the white paper again at this time
because it contains a thoughtful discussion of and recommendations regarding the appointment of individuals to the most critical sub-cabinet level jobs where science and technology is
central to a particular departmental or agency mission. We hope
that you will find the document useful as you participate in the
Presidential appointments process.

                          Yours sincerely,

Frank Press   Robert M. White   Kenneth I. Shine
President   President   President
National Academy   National Academy   Institute of
   of Sciences   of Engineering   Medicine

Enclosure

SCIENCE AND TECHNOLOGY LEADERSHIP IN AMERICAN GOVERNMENT

Ensuring the Best Presidential Appointments

A White Paper from the

NATIONAL ACADEMY OF SCIENCES
NATIONAL ACADEMY OF ENGINEERING
INSTITUTE OF MEDICINE

December 1992

EXECUTIVE SUMMARY

The new administration has emphasized the promise of science and technology (S&T) in helping to meet the social and economic challenges facing the Nation. To help deliver on this promise, it will be necessary to recruit approximately 78 outstanding and technically qualified individuals to top S&T positions in the federal government. Although they constitute only about twelve percent of presidentially appointed, Senate-confirmed positions, their successful recruitment will be critical to effective policymaking and management in key areas of government, including national security, energy, and health, to name only a few. To enhance the capacity of the executive branch to identify and recruit the very best people for these positions, the following measures should be undertaken:

- The President's Science Advisor should be appointed early, and one of his or her major tasks should be recruitment of outstanding scientists and engineers for key positions.

- The presidential personnel office should have specialized and experienced staff to work cooperatively with the Science Advisor and the department and agency heads in identifying and recruiting qualified appointees for S&T positions.

- Unnecessary barriers to hiring the best talent should be addressed early. Conflict-of-interest laws, especially those governing postgovernment employment, have become so complex and restrictive that they deter honest, public-minded scientists and engineers from serving. It is possible to have and administer conflict-of-interest laws in ways that protect the integrity of government and also meet the public's interest in having highly qualified and motivated scientists and engineers from industry and academia in the public service. Where necessary, existing provisions to exempt critically needed scientific and technological experts should be used.

- Recruitment for positions that are primarily technical will be much easier if they are not unduly politicized but are insulated from daily partisan pressures. Some S&T positions have term appointments in recognition that they are usually held by individuals appointed for the technical qualifications and judgment and that continuity of leadership in long-term S&T positions is desirable. Incumbents normally should be allowed to serve their full terms, unless their performance was below par or they have politicized their positions in a manner contrary to the administration's policy positions, and appointees in other primarily technical positions should be considered on a case-by-case basis rather than removed automatically.

SCIENCE AND TECHNOLOGY LEADERSHIP IN AMERICAN GOVERNMENT

Ensuring the Best Presidential Appointments

A White Paper from the

NATIONAL ACADEMY OF SCIENCES
NATIONAL ACADEMY OF ENGINEERING
INSTITUTE OF MEDICINE

December 1992

THE PROBLEM

There are approximately 78 top federal positions with important functional responsibilities in S&T policymaking and program management (see attached list). Although they constitute only about twelve percent of presidentially appointed, Senate-confirmed positions, the key S&T positions have an importance beyond their numbers on the Nation's ability to use science and technology to improve national security, public health, quality of life, and economic well-being.

In recent years, it has become increasingly difficult to fill such positions in a timely manner. This problem is most acute at the beginning of an administration, when many politically appointed positions must be filled in a very short period. The average time it takes to fill presidentially appointed positions has increased threefold since 1960. The average time from inauguration day to confirmation of PAS subcabinet positions was 2.4 months in the Kennedy administration, 5.3 months in the Reagan administration, and more than 8 months in the Bush administration. Some key positions took a year or more to fill—for example, the Director of the Office of Energy Research (22 months), the Director of the National Institutes of Health (18 months), and the Commissioner of the Food and Drug Administration (12 months). If the situation continues, the government's ability to make key decisions in the face of rapid scientific and technological change—and to design, carry out, and evaluate effective and responsive programs—will be seriously affected.

Recently the National Academies of Sciences and Engineering and the Institute of Medicine, with the support of the Carnegie Commission on Science, Technology, and Government, have studied the problems of recruitment and retention of science and engineering policy officials and have recommended steps to alleviate these problems. The study was conducted by a knowledgeable and experienced bipartisan group.[1]

---

[1] National Academy of Science, *Science and Technology Leadership in American Government: Ensuring the Best Presidential Appointments* (Washington, D.C.: National Academy Press, 1992). The bipartisan panel that prepared the report was chaired by Kenneth W. Dam. The members with White House or Executive Office of

CAUSAL FACTORS

Not only is it taking longer to fill key positions, especially at the beginning of new administrations, but it is also becoming harder to recruit top candidates. It has become less common to succeed in recruiting one of the top two or three candidates, and there have been cases where it was necessary to go to the tenth, twentieth, or even the thirtieth name on the list of desirable candidates. High turnover is also a concern. The Council for Excellence in Government found that the average tenure in top S&T positions is 2.5 years. These trends are disturbing because excellence and continuity are especially needed in S&T programs.

The factors making it harder to recruit highly qualified scientists, engineers, and medical experts for top government leadership include:

- More stringent and confusing postgovernment employment restrictions;
- The longer, more burdensome, and more intrusive nomination and Senate confirmation process;
- Stricter and more costly conflict-of-interest provisions;
- More detailed requirements for public financial disclosure;
- Pay that is not competitive with comparable positions in the private and nonprofit sectors;
- The high costs of moving to and living in Washington;
- Increased public scrutiny of one's personal life;
- Decreased capacity of government to carry out effective programs; and
- Lower public esteem for and prestige of public service.

AMELIORATING ACTIONS

There are three areas for action that can enable the government to attract the talent it needs for top science and engineering positions:

(1) improve the outreach to the science and engineering community and use more effective techniques for recruiting leading scientists and engineers.

(2) reduce the hurdles of the appointment process and the disincentives to government service.

President experience were Anne Wexler, James B. Wyngaarden, E. Pendleton James, and Charles Schultze; those who had held S&T leadership positions included John M. Deutch, John S. Foster, Robert C. Seamans, and Dr. Wyngaarden; those who had had department positions overseeing S&T policymaking and programs were R. James Woolsey, William T. Coleman, and Mr. Dam. The panel heard additional testimony from individuals knowledgeable about the problems of recruiting top candidates for S&T-related posts from past or current positions in the Executive Office of the President, including Lloyd Cutler and Elliot Richardson. Also, panel member J. Jackson Walter was the first director of the Office of Government Ethics.

(3) restructure certain positions to make them more attractive to scientists and engineers.

Improve Recruitment

The President's Science and Technology Advisor as Recruiter

Early designation of the President's Science Advisor will enable his or her active involvement in the effort to identify and recruit outstanding scientists and engineers for presidential appointments.

One of the key roles of the science advisor should be to assist the President in recruiting the best scientific and engineering talent in the country for top positions in the S&T-intensive agencies. In recent decades, however, presidential science advisors have been chosen too late to participate in the all-important initial recruitment effort of new administrations, and they have too seldom played a strong role in recruitment once they were on board. The importance of presidential leadership in attracting the best scientists and engineers for leadership positions in the executive branch cannot be overemphasized, and the selection and role of the President's Science Advisor is crucial to this perception. If the President's Science Advisor is of high stature in the research community and participates personally in presidential recruiting, the acceptance rate of the most qualified scientists and engineers would be increased.

Involvement of Departments and Agencies

A new administration not only must conduct the search and negotiation process required to fill 78 or so presidentially appointed S&T positions but also the other 470 full-time PAS jobs, nearly 2,350 additional full-time positions and several thousand part-time appointments to boards and commissions. **Without giving up their exclusive right to make executive appointments, presidents should place greater reliance on cabinet secretaries and agency heads for active identification and recruitment of candidates for subcabinet positions involving S&T expertise.** The White House and President's Science and Technology Advisor can concentrate on the highest priority positions while working cooperatively with the departments and agencies on the rest, scrutinizing the qualifications of those candidates put forth by Cabinet officers and agency heads.

The White House cannot hope directly to fill the thousands of PAS and other political positions that must be filled at the beginning of an administration in a timely fashion or thoroughly supervise them thereafter. In any case, most appointed S&T positions are level IV or V, are primarily specialized in nature, and work primarily with department leadership, not the White House. The White House office of presidential appointments is likely to be under intense pressure to fill positions for political reasons, while department and agency heads have a large stake in filling S&T positions with people of high expertise. They are also better able to match the person with the job, and they are more likely than the White House presidential appointments office to be connected to the networks in which technical experts operate professionally.

A Special S&T Unit in the White House Personnel Office

Because some of the best scientists and engineers do not think of seeking a presidentially appointed position and have to be actively recruited, **the White House office of presidential appointments should have a special unit charged with assisting in the recruiting of outstanding scientists and engineers, and it should be given sufficient resources to ensure a high level of professionalism in recruitment.**

The most qualified scientists and engineers are probably not looking for appointed positions in the government. They are less likely to be living in the Washington area already or to be involved in partisan politics than are capable individuals outside the S&T community. It is essential to reach out actively to this special, limited pool of potential appointees. Also, in some recent cases, initial contacts with prestigious scientists and engineers have not been well handled, leading potential candidates to believe that inappropriate criteria were being used or that political criteria, while appropriate to some degree, were being overemphasized relative to technical qualifications.

It is necessary and appropriate for the presidential appointments office in the White House to manage the overall confirmation process. A specialized and experienced staff unit, working in conjunction with the President's Science Advisor and concerned department and agency heads, would help the departments and agencies better perform the recruitment function.

Reduce Hurdles and Disincentives

The hurdles and disincentives in the presidential appointment process have become an ordeal that fewer and fewer of the most highly qualified scientists and engineers are willing to undergo. Some of the most important hurdles are conflict-of-interest laws that have proliferated. The integrity of government and public trust in government must be maintained, but, as a Nation, we also pay a high cost if top leadership positions are not filled by the most qualified and experienced experts.

Adopt Reasonable Conflict-of-Interest and Postgovernment Employment Restrictions

The unintended costs of broader conflict-of-interest restrictions—particularly those dealing with postgovernment employment of technical people—have reached the point where they substantially outweigh their benefits. It is possible to have fair and effective conflict-of-interest laws that are compatible with and would promote public service by highly qualified and motivated individuals from industry, academia, and other sectors.

Federal officials must not have conflicts of interest arising from financial or other personal interests in matters relating to their official duties or activities of their agencies. Federal officials are expected to serve the public interest, and they should not abuse their positions to enrich themselves, their families, or any organization in which they have a financial or personal interest.

Since the 1978 Ethics in Government Act set up the current procedures and established the Office of Government Ethics, cases where it has been impossible to resolve conflicts have been rare. Over time, however, there has been a natural tendency to resort to the most stringent "cure"—for example, divestiture and recusal.

In applying the conflict-of-interest laws, divestiture of assets should not be considered the primary remedy and therefore required routinely. Recusal, coupled with full public financial disclosure, should be considered by the Senate, the Office of Government Ethics, and designated agency ethics officials as the primary remedy in most cases. In many cases, recusal alone should be a sufficient remedy. If divestiture is necessary, it should not be coupled with recusal (unless the appointee retains some interest, such as pension rights). The public interest is better served if the least drastic—and least costly—remedy is used in each case, because it would improve recruitment of needed personnel.

Recent efforts to create a scandal-proof government have gone so far that, on balance, they may be doing more harm than good by deterring talented and experienced scientific and engineering personnel from taking senior government positions. Where laws afford little additional ethical protection at very high cost, they are a bad bargain for the government and the public. **Postemployment restrictions should be revised to balance the public's interest in ensuring the integrity of government operations with its interest in attracting the best talent to government service. At the same time, federal ethics laws, including postemployment restrictions, should be streamlined and clarified, and they should be contained in a single comprehensive section of the U.S. Code. To accomplish this, appropriate legislation should be submitted as soon as possible.**

In the meantime, since the new administration must conduct its initial and most important recruitment under existing laws, which are overlapping, conflicting, confusing, and in some respects overly broad, it should **make full use of current provisions for waivers and exemptions from the postemployment laws that apply to critically needed scientific and technological experts to the fullest extent needed. In certain cases, this will require personal approval of the President.**

Reduce the Disincentives to Government Service

The executive pay situation has eased considerably but will deteriorate again unless there are regular cost-of-living adjustments. The costs of entering the government service and staying there for an effective period of time, say four years, should be reasonable. This does not mean that the pay of appointees need be comparable to the private sector, but appointees should be able to meet their living costs. This principle may be more important for midcareer scientists and engineers than for other professionals, because they are not as likely to have accumulated much wealth and their government service will probably not boost their salaries as much after they leave government. **The President and Congress should ensure that there are regular salary reviews and pay increases, when justified by cost-of-living data, to avoid the large lapse in adequacy of executive pay that developed in the mid-1980s.**

Also, **the pay-related flexibilities authorized by the Federal Employees Pay Comparability Act of 1990 should be used selectively where necessary to recruit and keep top candidates for key positions.** These flexibilities include recruitment bonuses and retention allowances, special pay categories, and reimbursement for moving expenses.

Streamline Administrative Actions

The appointment process itself has become too elaborate and lengthy. This unnecessarily deters some potential candidates and hinders effective leadership. The sheer length and paperwork burden of the appointment process itself should be reduced. For example, background investigations of prospective nominees by the FBI add weeks and even months to the appointment process. To eliminate this source of significant delay, **the President could direct the FBI only to conduct background investigations since the last such investigation, where one exists.**

Nominees for PAS positions must fill out a series of separate, complicated, and incompatible financial disclosure and personal data forms for the Office of Personnel Management, the Office of Government Ethics, the FBI, and the White House and for the relevant Senate committee. This slows the process, imposes unnecessary legal and accounting costs on candidates, and multiplies the chance of error. **The administration should work with the relevant Senate committees to simplify and standardize forms and coordinate procedures used in the confirmation process.**

Make Jobs More Attractive

The positions can be made more attractive to top scientists and engineers, chiefly by ensuring that incumbents, once appointed, can see that their expert knowledge and judgment are heard and coupled effectively with S&T policymaking and management decisionmaking.

Unfortunately, there has been a growing belief in the scientific and engineering communities that the PAS jobs are becoming more difficult to do well. This belief stems in part from a perception that technical expertise and judgment are not given their due weight in making policy—or, sometimes, in making the appointments themselves. There have been many reports in recent decades (especially those associated with ideological or "litmus test" rejections of qualified potential nominees) that send a message that an incumbent's technical integrity may be compromised. There is also a perception that some positions have been pushed down too many layers in the decisionmaking structure to be effective.

Politics cannot and should not be removed from the top S&T jobs. S&T appointees, like all presidential appointees, should be willing and able to support the President's policy positions. But the President is served if the best technical judgment on difficult public policy issues is heard, considered, and balanced with other considerations by decisionmakers. The basic function of presidentially appointed S&T leaders is to bring technical knowledge and informed judgment to the policy arena and to foster policies that are defensible on *both* political and technical grounds. It follows that other considerations should not be permitted to prevail—in reality or perception—without the scientific and technical considerations being carefully considered.

There are ways to help ensure that technical expertise is heard and appropriately considered at top decisionmaking levels, and this would help to improve the attractiveness of S&T positions. For example, some positions have fixed terms and normally carry over from one administration to the next. These include the Surgeon General of the Public Health Service, the Director of the Bureau of Labor Statistics, the Director of the National Science Foundation, and the Chief Medical Director of the Department of Veterans Affairs. Fixed terms also promote continuity in policy and program management, which is often appropriate for S&T programs because they are typically long-term. **For these reasons, incumbents of such positions who were chosen primarily for their technical qualifications should be allowed to serve their full terms, unless their performance was below par or they have politicized their positions in a manner contrary to the President's policy positions.**

The political status, responsibilities and authorities, and reporting relationships of the government's top S&T positions should be reviewed periodically—and restructured as necessary—to ensure that the unbiased scientific and engineering judgment of incumbents is preserved and is directly introduced into the policy process. Such a process would help maintain the effectiveness and relevance of these important positions, which in turn would ensure that highly qualified and capable individuals would want to serve in them. The reviews should be a responsibility of the President's Science Advisor, with staff assistance from the Office of Science and Technology Policy. Independent reviews should also be conducted periodically by a private organization or set of organizations concerned with the government's effectiveness in carrying out its scientific and engineering missions.

Certain positions could be elevated in level and status to reduce "layering" and make them more effective in carrying out their responsibilities and thus more attractive to outstanding candidates. Some positions would be more attractive to highly qualified scientists and engineers if they were not subject to the presidential appointment process at all, but were filled through merit procedures. This was done successfully in the case of the assistant directors of the National Science Foundation, because political recruitment was taking too much time of the director and promising candidates were put off by the ordeal of the confirmation process in order to fill what they considered to be a professional position.

Finally, **working with the Congress, the President should carry out an overall reduction in political appointees (especially in Schedule C and noncareer Senior Executive Service jobs, but also in PAS positions), as recommended by the National Commission on the Public Service and other bipartisan and nonpartisan groups.**

The proliferation of political appointees is part of the problem in effective governance. Political layering and excessive interference from Schedule C and political SES appointees who work for higher level officials constitute important disincentives for highly competent individuals to serve. This is especially a problem in the S&T policy and administration area, because too much layering of authority affects the input of technical considerations in decisionmaking.

PRESIDENTIALLY APPOINTED SCIENCE- AND TECHNOLOGY-RELATED POSITIONS

Unit Position Title	Executive Pay Level

Executive Office of the President

Office of Science and Technology Policy

Assistant to the President for Science and Technology	II
Associate Director for Policy and International Affairs	III
Associate Director for Life Sciences	III
Associate Director for Physical Sciences and Engineering	III
Associate Director for Industrial Technology	III

Council of Economic Advisors

Chairman	II

Council on Environmental Quality

Chairman	IV

Departments

Agriculture

Assistant Secretary for Science and Education	IV

Commerce

Under Secretary, Technology	III
Assistant Secretary, Technology Policy	IV
Director, Census Bureau	IV
Assistant Secretary/Administrator, National Telecommunications and Information Administration	IV
Director, National Institute of Standards and Technology	IV
Under Secretary/Administrator, National Oceanic and Atmospheric Administration (NOAA)	III
Assistant Secretary, Oceans and Atmosphere	IV
Chief Scientist, NOAA	V

Defense

Director, Operational Test and Evaluation	IV
Under Secretary for Acquisition	II
Principal Deputy Under Secretary for Acquisition	III
Assistant to the Secretary of Defense (Atomic Energy)	V
Director of Defense Research and Engineering	IV
Assistant Secretary (Command, Control, Communications, and Intelligence)	IV
Assistant Secretary (Health Affairs)	IV

Air Force

Assistant Secretary (Acquisition)	IV

Army

Assistant Secretary (Research, Development and Acquisition)	IV

Navy

Assistant Secretary (Research, Development and Acquisition)	IV

Education
Assistant Secretary for Educational Research and Improvement — IV

Energy
Director, Civilian Radioactive Waste Management — IV
Assistant Secretary for Environment, Safety and Health — IV
Assistant Secretary for Conservation and Renewable Energy — IV
Director, Office of Alcohol Fuels — IV
Director, Office of Energy Research — IV
Assistant Secretary for Defense Programs — IV
Assistant Secretary for Nuclear Energy — IV
Assistant Secretary for Fossil Energy — IV
Administrator, Energy Information Service — IV

Health and Human Services
Assistant Secretary for Health — IV
Surgeon General, Public Health Service — PHS
Administrator, Alcohol, Drug Abuse, and Mental Health Administration — IV
Director, National Institutes of Health — IV
Director, National Cancer Institute — PA
Commissioner, Food and Drug Administration — IV

Housing and Urban Development
Assistant Secretary for Policy Development and Research — IV

Interior
Assistant Secretary—Fish and Wildlife, and Parks — IV
Director, U.S. Fish and Wildlife Service — V
Assistant Secretary for Water and Science — IV
Commissioner, Bureau of Reclamation — V
Director, Bureau of Mines — V
Director, U.S. Geological Survey — V

Justice
Director, Bureau of Justice Statistics — IV

Labor
Commissioner of Labor Statistics — V
Assistant Secretary for Occupational Safety and Health — IV
Assistant Secretary for Mine Safety and Health — IV

State
Under Secretary for International Security Affairs — III
Assistant Secretary, Oceans and International Environmental and Scientific Affairs — IV
Under Secretary for Economic Affairs — III

Transportation
Administrator, Federal Aviation Administration — II
Deputy Administrator, Federal Aviation Administration — IV
Administrator, National Highway Traffic Safety Administration — III

Veterans Affairs
Chief Medical Director — III

Independent Agencies

Agency for International Development
Assistant Administrator, Science and Technology   IV
Consumer Product Safety Commission
Chairman   III
Environmental Protection Agency
Administrator   II
Deputy Administrator   III
Assistant Administrator for Water   IV
Assistant Administrator for Solid Waste and Emergency Response   IV
Assistant Administrator for Air and Radiation   IV
Assistant Administrator for Pesticides and Toxic Substances   IV
Assistant Administrator for Research and Development   IV
National Aeronautics and Space Administration
Administrator   II
Deputy Administrator   III
National Science Foundation
Director   II
Deputy Director   III
National Transportation Safety Board
Chairman   III
Nuclear Regulatory Commission
Chairman   II
Tennessee Valley Authority
Chairman   III
U.S. Arms Control and Disarmament Agency
Assistant Director, Verification and Implementation   IV
Assistant Director, Nonproliferation Policy   IV

NOTE: The list includes the 50 PAS positions profiled in the Council for Excellence in Government's recent publication, *The Prune Book: The 60 Toughest Science and Technology Jobs in Washington*, by John H. Trattner (Lanham, Maryland: Madison Books, 1992). The list also includes 34 PAS positions beyond those listed by the CEG. In most cases these are positions *under* those profiled in the Prune Book. Neither list includes cabinet secretaries (executive level I) or deputy secretary positions (level II).

II

CLIMATE CHANGE POLICY

Establishing United States Leadership
Under the Climate Change Convention

NATIONAL ACADEMY OF SCIENCES
NATIONAL ACADEMY OF ENGINEERING
INSTITUTE OF MEDICINE

February 12, 1993

The Honorable Albert Gore, Jr.
Vice President of the United States
1600 Pennsylvania Avenue, N.W.
Washington, D.C.   20500

Dear Mr. Vice President:

As you well know, the threat of global climate change is perhaps the preeminent environmental problem of our time, one for which responses are urgently needed. In 1989, Congress asked the National Academy of Sciences, National Academy of Engineering, and Institute of Medicine to establish a blue ribbon panel to assess the issues surrounding greenhouse warming and to recommend actions to reduce the rate of warming and deal with its consequences. In 1991, we issued a summary of the panel's recommendations regarding mitigation and adaptation options, entitled: <u>Policy Implications of Greenhouse Warming</u>, and in 1992 we published a detailed supporting evaluation. Also in 1992, of course, leaders from 155 countries signed a climate change convention intended to reduce or offset emissions of greenhouse gases.

In the months before the Earth Summit, the Academies' panel assessed various ways of reducing emissions and the preparations needed to cope with climate change if it occurs. The panel concluded that the threat of greenhouse warming justifies action now. It recommended establishing a program to mitigate further buildup of greenhouse gases and initiate adaptation measures that are judicious and practical. The panel found that the United States could reduce its greenhouse gas emissions by between 10 and 40 percent of the 1990 level at very low cost. At the same time, a strong scientific program is needed to reduce the many uncertainties in our understanding of greenhouse warming and its effects on human and natural systems. In all of these efforts, international cooperation is essential.

A balanced, thoughtful, and well-founded approach, such as that developed by the Academies' expert panel, is essential if progress is to be made on this problem, while at the same time increasing jobs and stimulating economic

growth.   Implementing these recommendations would also help
to establish the United States leadership in fulfilling the
provisions of the climate change convention.   We hope,
therefore, that you will take the time to review this brief
summary of the key findings and recommendations of the
Academies' report.

Yours sincerely,

Frank Press
President
National Academy
of Sciences

Robert M. White
President
National Academy
of Engineering

Kenneth I. Shine
President
Institute of
Medicine

Enclosure

CLIMATE CHANGE POLICY

Establishing United States Leadership under the Climate Change Convention

A White Paper from the

NATIONAL ACADEMY OF SCIENCES
NATIONAL ACADEMY OF ENGINEERING
INSTITUTE OF MEDICINE

February 1993

The Earth Summit in Rio de Janeiro established global environmental problems as a central challenge in the post-Cold War world. At that event, leaders from 155 countries signed an unprecedented climate change convention intended to reduce or offset emissions of greenhouse gases and thus avoid the threat of excessive global warming. In the months before the Earth Summit, a special panel established by the National Academy of Sciences, the National Academy of Engineering, and the Institute of Medicine assessed ways of reducing emissions and the preparations needed to cope with climate change if it occurs.[1]

THE THREAT OF CLIMATE CHANGE

Greenhouse warming--a rise in global average temperature due to increasing atmospheric concentrations of greenhouse gases--represents a new kind of global environmental problem that will likely continue to grow in importance. It is universally agreed that atmospheric concentrations of greenhouse gases have increased over the last 100 years and continue to increase due to the burning of fossil fuels, deforestation, and other industrial and agricultural

---

[1]The Panel on Policy Implications of Greenhouse Warming consisted of: the Honorable Daniel J. Evans (chair), Robert McCormick Adams, George F. Carrier, Richard N. Cooper, Robert A. Frosch, Thomas H. Lee, Jessica Tuchman Mathews, William D. Nordhaus, Gordon H. Orians, Stephen H. Schneider, Maurice F. Strong, Sir Crispin Tickell, Victoria J. Tschinkel, and Paul E. Waggoner. The findings and recommendations presented here are described in more detail in the panel's report Policy Implications of Greenhouse Warming: Mitigation, Adaptation, and the Science Base (National Academy Press, Washington, D.C.: 1992). The estimates of the cost-effectiveness of mitigation options have been updated in E.S. Rubin et al., "Realistic Mitigation Options for Global Warming," Science (257)148-149,261-268.

activities. During the same period, the global surface temperature has increased about one degree Fahrenheit. It is impossible to demonstrate scientifically whether or not this increase in global average temperature is due to increased concentrations of greenhouse gases.

Despite uncertainties, there is widespread agreement that anthropogenic greenhouse gas emissions will eventually raise the global average temperature. Feedback mechanisms and other events such as volcanic eruptions or the emission of tropospheric aerosols can counter global warming, but likely only temporarily. Continued increases in emissions of greenhouse gases have the potential to produce a planet warmer than at any time in human experience. However, the rate of this temperature increase and the implications of warming for various regions are not well known, which makes it difficult to determine the exact consequences of global warming.

In estimating the likely impacts of greenhouse warming, **it is not only necessary to project climatic conditions many years into the future. Adjustments by human and natural ecosystems must also be taken into account.** Farmers adjust their behavior in response to changing weather patterns, as do plants and animals. A proper analysis of the impacts of greenhouse warming must also account for adjustments in national and regional economies as well as in other human and natural systems.

Because the United States is a large country with many intellectual and material resources and a wide range of climatic zones, it is better prepared to cope with the consequences of climate change than are less well-endowed countries. Nevertheless, the necessary adjustments are not without economic and social costs, and economically sound measures need to be adopted that can reduce possible adverse consequences.

The greatest sensitivities to greenhouse warming in the United States derive from the limited capacities of ecosystems to adapt to climate change. Depending on the rapidity of the climatic changes and the ability of ecosystem components to migrate or adapt to new conditions, significant ecosystem stresses could arise with as yet unknown consequences. Another threat stems from possible sea level rise and saltwater incursion into coastal areas. The less we are willing to accept the risk of such future conditions, the greater our motivation to reduce or offset emissions today and take other precautionary measures.

If the climate does change, other countries will face greater difficulties than will the United States, especially poor countries or those with fewer and marginal climate zones. For example, cereal production probably will decrease in some of the currently high-production areas and increase in other regions, which will alter patterns of agricultural trade (although total global food production probably can be maintained at essentially the same level as would have occurred without climate change). Recognition that poor countries may both bear a greater burden and have less resources to cope was a major factor in the negotiations leading to the climate change convention.

THE CONTEXT FOR INTERNATIONAL AND DOMESTIC ACTION

Projections suggest that greenhouse gas emissions in developing countries will exceed those from the industrialized countries sometime early in the next century. Most of the increases in greenhouse gas emissions have been a product of the efforts of people to secure improved standards of food, clothing, shelter, comfort, and recreation. Rapidly growing populations and the pressure to develop their economies have led developing countries to substantially increase their emissions of greenhouse gases, just as emissions from the industrialized countries have continued to rise.

Although there clearly is a relationship between population, economic activity, and climate change, it is not a simple one. Increasing population is one of the major factors affecting trends in greenhouse gas emissions. More people create greater demand for food, energy, clothing, and shelter. Producing such products emits greenhouse gases. Economic growth also produces more greenhouse gases. Many nations have policies to reduce population growth rates, but all nations seek to achieve rapid growth in per capita income. The reduction of greenhouse gas emissions is well served by the first objective but, depending on the means used, can be in conflict with the second.

REDUCING OR OFFSETTING GREENHOUSE GAS EMISSIONS

Major greenhouse gases emitted by human activities include carbon dioxide, methane, chlorofluorocarbons (CFCs), hydrogenated chlorofluorocarbons (HCFCs), ozone, and nitrous oxide. Figure 1 shows different ways to reduce or offset these emissions ranked in order of their cost-effectiveness. The most cost-effective option (residential and commercial energy efficiency), if fully implemented, could reduce emissions by about 11 percent at a net savings of about $62 per ton. The second most cost-effective option (vehicle efficiency with no change in fleet attributes) could produce an additional 4 percent reduction in emissions at a net savings of about $40 per ton.

	Net Implementation Cost ($/t CO_2 equivalent)	Maximum Potential Emission Reduction (Gt CO_2 eq./yr.)	Percent Reduction in U.S. Emissions CO_2 eq. (%)
1 Resid. & Comm. Energy Efficiency	-62	0.9	11
2 Vehicle Efficiency (no fleet change)	-40	0.3	4
3 Industrial Electric Efficiency	-25	0.5	7
4 Transportation System Management	-22	0.05	1
5 Power Plant Heat Rate Improvements	0	0.05	1
6 Landfill Gas Collection	1	0.2	3
7 Halocarbons	1	1.4	18
8 Agriculture	3	0.2	3
9 Reforestation	7	0.2	3
10 Electricity Supply	45	1.0	13

FIGURE 1 Mid-cost comparison of mitigation options, assuming 100 percent implementation

Overall, **the United States could reduce its greenhouse gas emissions by between 10 and 40 percent of the 1990 level (depending on the extent of implementation of each option) at very low cost.** Some reductions may even be at a net savings if the proper policies are implemented. Implementation of the most cost-effective options would place the United States in a position of world leadership in the response to the threat of greenhouse warming.

Three general areas with the greatest promise of reducing or offsetting current emissions are: changing energy policy, eliminating halocarbon emissions, and using forest offsets.

Energy Policy

The United States can reduce emissions of greenhouse gases by enhancing energy conservation and efficiency. Potential actions include:

- Adopt nationwide energy-efficient building codes
- Improve the efficiency of the U.S. automotive fleet through the use of an appropriate combination of regulation and tax incentives
- Strengthen federal and state support of mass transit
- Improve appliance efficiency standards
- Encourage public education and information programs for conservation and recycling
- Reform state public utility regulation to encourage electrical utilities to promote efficiency and conservation
- Sharply increase the emphasis on efficiency and conservation in the federal energy research and development budget

- Use federal and state purchases of goods and services to demonstrate "best practice" technologies and energy conservation programs

The efficiency of practically every end use of energy can be improved relatively inexpensively. Major reductions could be achieved in energy use in existing buildings through improvements in lighting, water heating, refrigeration, space heating and cooling, and cooking. Gains could be achieved in transportation by improving vehicle efficiency without downsizing or altering convenience. Significant gains could be achieved in industrial electricity use through fuel switching and improvements in process technologies.

Initial calculations show that some options could be implemented at a net savings. There are informational barriers to overcome, however. For example, homeowners may not be aware of the gains to be realized from high-efficiency furnaces. There are also institutional barriers. For example, most public utility commissions disallow a rate of return to power companies on efficiency and conservation options. The panel concluded that energy efficiency and conservation is a rich field for reducing greenhouse gas emissions.

The United States can make greenhouse warming a key factor in planning for our future energy supply mix. A systems approach should be adopted that considers the interactions among supply, conversion, end use, and external effects in improving the economics and performance of the overall energy system. Action items include efforts to:

- Develop combined cycle systems that have efficiencies approaching 60 percent for both coal- and natural-gas-fired plants
- Encourage broader use of natural gas by identifying and removing obstacles in the distribution system
- Develop and test operationally a new generation of nuclear reactor technology that is designed to deal with safety, waste management, and public acceptability
- Increase research and development on alternative energy supply technologies (e.g., solar), and design energy systems using them in conjunction with other energy supply technologies to optimize economy and performance
- Accelerate efforts to assess the economic and technical feasibility of carbon dioxide sequestration from fossil-fuel-based generating plants

The future energy supply mix will change as new energy technologies and greenhouse warming take on increased importance. A systems approach should be used to optimize the economics and performance of future energy systems. Interactions among supply options, conversion systems, end use, and external effects should receive much more attention than they have in the past. Actions for improving energy supply systems must cover all important elements in the mix. Also, it is important to prepare for the possibility that greenhouse warming may become far more serious in the future.

Alternative energy technologies are unable currently or in the near future to replace fossil fuels as the major electricity source for this country. If fossil fuels had to be replaced now as the primary source of electricity, nuclear power appears to be the most technically feasible alternative. But nuclear reactor designs capable of meeting fail-safe criteria and satisfying public concerns have not yet been demonstrated. A new generation of reactor design is needed that adequately addresses the full range of safety, waste management, economic, and other issues confronting nuclear power. Focused research and development work on a variety of alternative energy supply sources could result in large changes in future energy supplies.

U.S. institutions need to explore modes of social cost pricing of energy, with a goal of gradually introducing such a system.

On the basis of the principle that the polluter should pay, pricing of energy production and use should in an ideal world reflect the costs of the associated environmental problems. The concept of social cost pricing is a goal toward which to strive, but much research remains to be conducted on how to achieve or approximate this goal. Including all social, environmental, and other costs in energy prices would provide consumers and producers with the appropriate information to decide about fuel mix, new investments, and research and development. Phasing such a policy in over time is essential to avoid shocks caused by rapid price changes. It would best be coordinated internationally.

Halocarbon Emissions

The United States should continue the aggressive phaseout of CFC and other halocarbon emissions and the development of substitutes that minimize or eliminate greenhouse gas emissions.

Although estimates of the contribution of halocarbon emissions to greenhouse warming recently have been reduced, these substitutes continue to contribute to the depletion of stratospheric ozone. The 1987 Montreal Protocol, and the subsequent agreements reached in London and Berlin, set goals regarding the international phaseout of CFC manufacture and emissions. These agreements should be forcefully implemented.

Forest Offsets

Global deforestation needs to be reduced. The United States and other countries should:

- Participate in international programs to assess the extent of deforestation, especially in tropical regions, and to develop effective action plans to slow or halt deforestation.
- Undertake country-by-country programs of technical assistance or other incentives.
- Review domestic policies to remove subsidies and other incentives contributing to deforestation.

In addition to reducing the uptake of carbon dioxide in plants and soils and being a source of atmospheric carbon dioxide, deforestation contributes to other important problems: loss of species and reduction in the diversity of biologic systems, soil erosion, decreased capacity to retain water in soil and altered runoff of rainfall, and alteration of local weather patterns. The United States now has increasing forest cover, but tropical forests worldwide are being lost at a rapid rate. Nearly every aspect of tropical deforestation, however, is difficult to measure.

Even the amount of land deforested each year is subject to disagreement. Nevertheless, action should be initiated now to slow and eventually halt tropical deforestation. Such programs need to be developed by those countries where the affected forests are located in cooperation with other countries and international organizations. Developing countries with extensive tropical forests will require substantial technological and developmental aid if this goal is to be reached.

The United States should explore a moderate domestic reforestation program and support international reforestation efforts.

Reforestation offers the potential of offsetting a large amount of carbon dioxide emissions, but at a cost that increases sharply as the amount of offset increases. These costs include not only those of implementation, but also the loss of other productive uses of the land planted to forests, such as land for food production. Reforesting can, at best, only remove carbon dioxide from the atmosphere and store it during the lifetime of the trees. When a forest matures, the net uptake of carbon dioxide stops. If the reforested areas are then harvested, the only true offset of carbon dioxide buildup is the amount of carbon stored as lumber or other long-lived products. However, the wood might be used as a sustained-yield energy crop to replace fossil fuel use. The acreage available within the United States for reforestation, and the amount of carbon dioxide that could be captured on these lands with appropriate kinds of trees, are controversial and may be limited. Many details remain to be resolved.

ENHANCING ADAPTATION TO GREENHOUSE WARMING IN THE UNITED STATES

Human societies and natural systems of plants and animals change over time and react to changing climate just as they react to other forces. It would be fruitless to try to maintain all human and natural communities in their current forms. There are actions that can be taken now, however, to help people and natural systems adjust to some of the anticipated impacts of greenhouse warming by increasing resilience to climate change. Moreover, as noted previously, the Academy panel concluded that in all likelihood the United States can probably adapt and adjust without great difficulty.

Helping Human Systems Adapt

An effective way to reduce vulnerability to future climate change is to **make affected human systems more robust to current variations in climate.** Specific actions include:

- Maintain basic, applied, and experimental agricultural research to help farmers and commerce adapt to climate change and thus ensure ample food.
- Make water supply more robust by coping with present variability. Efficiency of use should be increased by greater reliance on water markets and by better management of present systems of supply.
- Plan margins of safety for long-lived structures to take into consideration possible climate change.

Helping Natural Systems Adapt

Any future climate change is likely to increase the current rate of loss of biodiversity while at the same time increasing the value of genetic resources. **Greenhouse warming therefore adds urgency to programs to preserve our biological heritage.** Even without greenhouse warming, steps are warranted to slow present losses in biodiversity. Specific actions that should be taken include:

- Establish and manage areas encompassing full ranges of habitats
- Inventory little-known organisms and sites
- Collect key organisms in repositories such as seed banks
- Search for new active compounds in wild plants and animals
- Control and manage wild species to avoid over-exploitation
- Pursue captive breeding and propagation of valuable species that have had their habitats usurped or populations drastically reduced
- Review policies, laws, and administrative procedures that have the effect of promoting species destruction
- Consider purchasing land or easements suitable for helping vulnerable species to migrate to new habitats

IMPROVING KNOWLEDGE FOR FUTURE DECISIONS

Data collection and research can contribute to reducing the uncertainties of greenhouse warming. The return on investment in research is likely to be great. Actions should be taken in the following areas:

- Continue and expand the collection and dissemination of data that provide an uninterrupted record of the evolving climate and of data that are (or will become) needed for the improvement and testing of climate models.
- Improve weather forecasts, especially of extremes, for weeks and seasons to ease adaptation to climate change.
- Continue to identify those mechanisms that play a significant role in the climatic response to changing concentrations of greenhouse gases. Develop and/or improve quantification of all such mechanisms at a scale appropriate for climate models.
- Conduct field research on entire systems of species over many years to learn how carbon dioxide enrichment alters the mix of species and changes the total production or quality of biomass. Research should be accelerated to determine how greenhouse warming might affect biodiversity.
- Strengthen research on social and economic aspects of global change and greenhouse warming.
- Undertake research and development projects to improve our understanding of both the potential of large-scale "geoengineering" options for reducing or offsetting global

warming and their possible side-effects. This is not a recommendation that geoengineering options be undertaken at this time, but rather that we learn more about their likely advantages and disadvantages.

EXERCISING INTERNATIONAL LEADERSHIP

As the largest source of current greenhouse gas emissions, the United States should exercise leadership in addressing responses to greenhouse warming.

The United States should participate fully with officials at an appropriate level in international agreements and in programs to address greenhouse warming, including diplomatic conventions and research and development efforts.

The United States should participate fully in mechanisms for implementing the climate change convention and continue its active scientific role in related topics. The global character of greenhouse warming provides a special opportunity in the area of research and development. International cooperation in research and development should be encouraged through governmental and private sector agreements. International organizations providing funds for development should be encouraged to evaluate projects meeting demand for energy growth by conservation methods on an equal footing with projects entailing construction of new production capacity.

PROMOTING THE CONTROL OF POPULATION GROWTH

In addition, control of population growth has the potential to make a major contribution to raising living standards and to easing environmental problems like greenhouse warming. The United States should resume full participation in international programs to slow population growth and should contribute its share to their financial and other support.[2]

Population size and economic activity both affect greenhouse gas emissions. Even with rapid technological advance, slowing global population growth is a necessary component of a long-term effort to control worldwide emissions of greenhouse gases. Reducing population growth alone, however, may not reduce emissions of greenhouse gases because it may also stimulate growth in per capita income. If the nature of economic activity (especially energy use) changes, some growth will be possible with far less greenhouse gas emissions.

Encouraging voluntary population control programs is of considerable benefit for slowing future emissions of greenhouse gases. In addition, countries vulnerable to the possible impacts of climate change would be better able to adapt to those changes if their populations were smaller and they had higher per capita income.

---

[2] The new Administration has already proposed and/or initiated a number of steps that will change the direction of U.S. population policy to be more responsive to concerns about global warming.

CONCLUDING COMMENTS

Even given the considerable uncertainties in our knowledge, **greenhouse warming poses a potential threat sufficient to merit prompt responses.** People in this country could probably adapt to the likely changes associated with greenhouse warming. The costs, however, could be substantial. **Investment in mitigation measures acts as insurance protection against the great uncertainties and the possibility of dramatic surprises.** In addition, substantial mitigation can be accomplished at modest cost. In other words, insurance is cheap. **Such insurance will be effective, however, only to the extent that mitigation options are implemented effectively.**

Implementation of the recommendations outlined here would establish the United States as a world leader in addressing environmental problems and would help fulfill the provisions of the climate change convention.

III

TECHNOLOGY POLICY AND INDUSTRIAL INNOVATION

The Federal Government's Role

NATIONAL ACADEMY OF SCIENCES
NATIONAL ACADEMY OF ENGINEERING
INSTITUTE OF MEDICINE

NATIONAL ACADEMY OF SCIENCES
NATIONAL ACADEMY OF ENGINEERING
INSTITUTE OF MEDICINE

2101 Constitution Avenue, Washington, D.C. 20418

February 12, 1993

The Honorable Albert Gore, Jr.
Vice President of the United States
1600 Pennsylvania Avenue, N.W.
Washington, D.C.   20500

Dear Mr. Vice President:

During the election campaign, President Clinton emphasized his deep commitment to promoting the industrial revitalization and international economic competitiveness of the United States. Clearly, one element of this initiative must be increased efforts to promote the development of new, commercializable technologies and the basic research that makes such breakthroughs possible. In the attached white paper, which was prepared for the Presidential transition on the basis of the recent report of the National Academy of Sciences, the National Academy of Engineering and the Institute of Medicine entitled: The Government Role in Civilian Technology: Building a New Alliance, it is pointed out that the government does have a legitimate role in promoting industrial innovation.

There is a sound economic rationale for federal action to promote both investment in pre-commercial R&D and technology adoption in U.S. firms. Private markets often fail to provide for sufficient levels of investment in these areas. Just as in basic research, government should facilitate private R&D investment in areas with high social rates of return and where firms cannot fully appropriate (capture) the economic benefits of R&D funding.

The white paper argues that, as part of a new federal technology policy, current federal programs in R&D should be strengthened. Specifically, (1) the Defense Advanced Research Projects Agency's role in dual-use technology development should be reaffirmed; (2) only a small number of the 700 federal laboratories, those which are most appropriately qualified, should be selected to work with private firms in technology transfer; (3) the scope of selected mission agency R&D programs should be enlarged to include pre-commercial projects; (4) the Advanced Technology

Program should be evaluated to determine the desirable size of the program, and; (5) current industrial extension services provided by the Commerce Department should be expanded to speed technology adoption in industry.

The paper suggests several organizational options for consideration by the Administration as it seeks to advance the technological capabilities of the nation, including the possibility of establishing a Civilian Technology Corporation, which was the option that the committee favored in the Academies' recent report.

The challenge of finding effective and appropriate ways for the U.S. Government to promote industrial innovation--and hence, U.S. international competitiveness--is both daunting and urgent. We hope that you will find that the enclosed white paper, and the longer report on which it is based, provides a number of useful and innovative ideas to assist the Administration in framing its policy response.

Yours sincerely,

Frank Press
President
National Academy
   of Sciences

Robert M. White
President
National Academy
   of Engineering

Kenneth I. Shine
President
Institute of
   Medicine

Enclosure

TECHNOLOGY POLICY AND INDUSTRIAL INNOVATION

The Federal Government's Role

A White Paper from the

NATIONAL ACADEMY OF SCIENCES
NATIONAL ACADEMY OF ENGINEERING
INSTITUTE OF MEDICINE

February 1993

As we approach the 21st century, national welfare will depend increasingly on federal policies that build on U.S. strengths in science and technology. Rapid economic growth, increased productivity, and improved standards of living require investments that leverage our comparative advantage in high technology. The federal government has a legitimate role in this process. At the same time, government policies must continue to safeguard the competitive dynamic and industrial efficiencies that market forces nurture.[1]

THE RATIONALE FOR CHANGE

By many measures, the United States remains strong in technology and continues to exhibit considerable industrial strength. We are the most productive nation in the world. Manufacturing output is increasing at a rapid rate. U.S. exports of high-technology manufactured goods are growing. As measured by indicators such as patents awarded and the balance of trade in high-technology goods and services, the innovative capacity of the United States remains unsurpassed.

Although the nation's technological performance is strong, this does not mean that U.S. policy should continue unaltered. The most important reason for a new technology policy, one that builds on our comparative strength in research and innovation, centers on productivity. The United States needs to improve its performance in all areas that promote productivity and long-

---

1 The National Academy of Sciences, National Academy of Engineering, and Institute of Medicine recently issued a report on technology policy, *The Government Role in Civilian Technology: Building a New Alliance.* The final report was prepared at the request of Congress in Public Law 100-418, and provides a useful framework and economic rationale for government investment in R&D.

term economic growth. Investment in R&D to achieve higher rates of technology commercialization and adoption should be a central part of the new administration's technology policy.

There is a sound economic rationale to support implementation of a federal strategy to facilitate industrial innovation. Government needs to create incentives for private investment in pre-commercial R&D beyond basic research in areas where firms cannot appropriate (capture) the economic benefits of investment. Just as the government acts to prevent underinvestment in basic research through federal funding, policymakers must recognize and should alleviate market failure downstream in pre-commercial R&D, as well.

STRENGTHENING CURRENT GOVERNMENT PROGRAMS

The first step in building a new alliance between government and industry in civilian technology is action to strengthen federal programs that facilitate private sector R&D, and the transfer or adoption of technology. Specifically,

- the Defense Advanced Research Projects Agency's role in dual-use technology development--especially in the area of information technology--should be reaffirmed;

- only a small number of the 700 federal laboratories, those which are most appropriately qualified, should be selected to work with private firms in an effort to enhance technology transfer;

- the scope of selected mission agency R&D programs should be enlarged to include pre-commercial projects;

- funding for the Small Business Innovation Research program should be increased;

- the Department of Commerce's Advanced Technology Program has had a promising start. It should be evaluated, by an independent group, to determine the desirable size of the program, and;

- current industrial extension services provided by the Commerce Department should be expanded to speed technology adoption in industry.

PROMOTING INVESTMENT IN PRE-COMMERCIAL R&D

A new technology strategy for the post-Cold War era must include more than revisions in current federal programs. The government should act to correct the failure of private markets to support pre-commercial R&D. Moreover, the ability of U.S. companies to adopt new technologies, an important part of economic growth, is weak. As in the case of pre-commercial R&D, private markets fail to provide sufficient levels of investment at this stage of the technology development process.

In basic science there is a clear need for federal funding. Companies have little incentive to invest in basic R&D, because in many cases research results are widely available and firms cannot capture the economic benefits of basic science investments.

Beyond basic research, there is an area of science and engineering work that precedes product- or process-specific, applied R&D. At this pre-commercial stage, private sector estimates of commercial market potential are uncertain and appropriability of the fruits of investment are unclear. Technical obstacles in moving to the applied research or prototype development stage are present as well. Pre-commercial R&D is also often characterized by spillovers into the general knowledge base, where other firms can appropriate the economic benefits of another firm's investments. This R&D constitutes a public good, one that merits government financial support. To be effective, government-industry R&D ventures with public sector support should be guided by a set of principles which should include:

(1) Cost-sharing provisions

Cost sharing is especially important in pre-commercial R&D programs. Cooperative R&D projects between government and industry should ensure that public funds are used to build on corporate strengths in technology. Direct, 100 percent government subsidies to private firms for R&D projects run the risk of redirecting scarce resources, both financial and human, into unproductive channels. To ensure the commercial relevance of R&D funded by the government through cooperative ventures, private sector firms or institutions should cover at least 50 percent of total project costs.

(2) Project initiation and design by private firms

The long-term objective of any government financial commitment to pre-commercial R&D should be to enhance private sector productivity. To do this, R&D must be linked to commercial markets and channeled into areas with the potential for wide industrial application. Collaborative R&D ventures funded through government-industry partnerships should be proposed and structured by industry.

(3) Insulation from political concerns

To minimize improper political influence in the allocation of government funds, projects to be supported by government should be based on technical and economic assessments of the merits of each project. Evaluations of competing R&D proposals should be conducted by independent experts in the relevant scientific, technological, and economic areas. Political considerations should not influence technical output, the location of R&D facilities, or the management of research projects.

(4) A diversified set of R&D objectives

A broad portfolio of investments in a wide range of technical fields, including the biomedical sciences and biotechnology, materials sciences, manufacturing product and process technologies, and computer and telecommunications-related technologies, among others, is important to the success of any technology strategy. A broad-based technology program will help to ensure that government-sponsored R&D does not become captive to the interests of a particular technology champion or a set of companies.

(5) Rigorous project evaluations and review

Detailed technical and economic evaluations are essential to any technology program, especially in pre-commercial R&D. Independent evaluation should be undertaken by non-governmental experts, including those with technical, managerial, and economic experience, in any new federal technology efforts. Current efforts to review government R&D programs are impeded, in some cases, because reports to Congress and president are often conducted by mission agency employees. These officials have a direct interest in ensuring the continuation of projects that they evaluate.

If the original objectives of a joint R&D venture sponsored with federal financial assistance are reached, or the results of a program do not justify the resources expended, programs should be automatically terminated. Federal agency officials and Congress should, as a matter of policy, follow recommendations by review panels, either to terminate or to extend a project.

(6) Projects open to foreign firms characterized by a substantial contribution to U.S. Gross Domestic Product (GDP)

Government should encourage the flow of technology and production capabilities of the most up-to-date and competitive kind to both U.S. and foreign corporations located within U.S. borders. There are significant benefits that accrue to the economy through the training, education, and skill enhancement offered by foreign-based corporations with U.S. affiliates, for example. Foreign-owned corporations located in the U.S. contribute directly to our national economic growth in other ways as well. One increasingly important contribution is through cooperative R&D work with U.S. firms.

Public policies that seek to close domestic markets to foreign goods and services, limit technology flows, or restrict foreign participation in government technology programs, therefore, damage U.S. economic interests. They serve to isolate the economy from scientific and technological advances made in other industrialized nations. Finally, it is important that U.S. firms gain access to foreign collaborative R&D programs and the benefits of participation in these ventures.

A CIVILIAN TECHNOLOGY CORPORATION

Many proposals have been introduced for organizing and managing federal technology investments in pre-commercial R&D. These include the creation of a new executive branch agency, or simply increasing current funding levels in existing agency budgets. Existing agency budgets should be selectively increased at agencies that have had success in past programs aimed at promoting commercial technology development efforts. This might include, for example, DARPA, the Department of Energy's support for energy research, and the National Institutes of Health.

Creation of a civilian technology agency, however, has several serious disadvantages. A technology agency would likely be dwarfed in size, budget, status, and influence by existing federal departments. Its establishment would face opposition from agencies and congressional committees anxious to guard prerogatives over technology areas. Unless its purpose were clearly defined and its authority affirmed, a new agency would add to the federal bureaucracy without achieving many concrete results. Moreover, a government technology agency would be subject to federal procurement guidelines, and civil service hiring rules, both of which would severely limit its effectiveness.

The most serious disadvantage of a civilian agency is its placement in the executive branch. This would increase the likelihood that support of projects would be influenced by special interest groups and parochial political concerns. An agency of the federal government, whether housed in an existing organization or independently controlled, would be a central part of the political process.

One effective way to promote substantial federal investment in pre-commercial R&D is through creation of a Civilian Technology Corporation (CTC). The goal of a CTC would be to increase the rate at which products and processes are commercialized in the U.S. This objective can be met by stimulating investment in the pre-commercial stage of technology development with high social rates of return, but where firms cannot appropriate sufficient benefits of R&D work. Higher levels of investment at this stage of the innovation process will, over the long term, translate into stronger U.S. performance in technology commercialization.

The CTC would be a quasi-governmental organization, funded through a one-time $5 billion congressional appropriation. A board of directors, appointed by the President and subject to Senate confirmation, would manage the corporation. The performance and operation of the CTC would undergo an independent review after the fourth and tenth years of operation.

IV

TOWARD MORE EFFECTIVE HEALTH CARE REFORM

Selected Issues from Reports of the Institute of Medicine

NATIONAL ACADEMY OF SCIENCES
INSTITUTE OF MEDICINE

February 10, 1993

The Honorable
Donna Shalala
Secretary
Department of Health and Human Services
Hubert H. Humphrey Building, Room 615F
200 Independence Avenue, S.W.
Washington, D.C. 20201

Dear Dr. Shalala:

The Institute of Medicine of the National Academy of Sciences has engaged its distinguished membership and other experts in analyses of many health policy issues directly relevant to health care reform. We share your and the Administration's desire to improve the health and well-being of all Americans. The enclosed paper Toward More Effective Health Care Reform cites conclusions and recommendations of some of our reports that should be helpful in the formulation of your specific plans for change. A more comprehensive list of germane IOM reports is appended to that paper.

We stand ready to work with you and your colleagues as you not only strive to achieve universal access to appropriate care and to moderate the increase in health care expenditures but also seek to improve the health and well-being for all Americans.

Sincerely,

Frank Press
President
National Academy of Sciences

Kenneth I. Shine
President
Institute of Medicine

Enclosure

TOWARD MORE EFFECTIVE HEALTH CARE REFORM

Selected Issues from Reports of the Institute of Medicine, National Academy of Sciences

A White Paper from the

NATIONAL ACADEMY OF SCIENCES
NATIONAL ACADEMY OF ENGINEERING
INSTITUTE OF MEDICINE

February 1993

TOWARD MORE EFFECTIVE HEALTH CARE REFORM

We commend your commitment to health care reform, an endeavor that poses significant challenges and opportunities to us all in the months ahead. Constraining the rapid escalation of health care costs while extending health insurance coverage to all, the primary objectives of reform, will require significant improvements in the performance of our system for health care, especially since some of the factors increasing health care expenditures, such as the aging of the population, are external to the health care system and will continue. We believe that achieving effective change must include concrete steps to assure: that services are appropriate and effective, that universal access is actually accomplished, that resources are used efficiently to realize improvements in health status, that health care professionals are trained and deployed appropriately, and that better information is marshalled to improve performance. We also believe that performance improvements should be measured by advances in the health and well-being of Americans in addition to relief of the economic burden.

Based on work that this organization has done on many health care issues, we believe that improved performance will call for:

- strengthening our capability to measure and continuously improve the quality of care;

- enhancing value in health care through better information about people's health status, the outcomes and effectiveness of medical care, and the application of that information in the development and use of clinical practice guidelines;

- addressing the special health needs of pregnant women and children, the frail elderly, people with AIDS, individuals with severe mental disorders, and of the poor, minorities, and other special populations that are unlikely to be met adequately through health insurance coverage alone;

- restructuring the health care system to place more emphasis on primary care and less on the use of specialized services;

- reducing the incentives for some payers to achieve cost savings by avoiding those with higher health risks; and

- providing the information and knowledge that are essential if we are to improve access, quality, and health status while restraining cost increases.

The Institute of Medicine (IOM) has produced several reports that address these objectives and contain specific, detailed recommendations, based on the careful deliberations of committees of distinguished experts. (A list of the reports relevant to health care reform is appended to this paper.) In this paper, we highlight how the recommendations in these reports can help health care reform achieve greater impact on health status and greater efficiency in the use of resources devoted to health care, with special attention to four main topics:

- quality assessment and improvement;
- the value of health care;
- special populations: children and pregnant women; and
- health care data and information.

These four topics, together with universal access and cost containment, are not the only objectives that a health care reform package ought to embrace. Indeed, a parallel commitment to health promotion and disease prevention will be essential for improving the health and well-being of all Americans, and for some health problems will be more important than health and health care reform *per se*. In fact, the IOM has examined many other relevant topics over the years, including matters relating to the future of public health (IOM, 1988) and the nation's health goals for the year 2000 (IOM, 1990e). In our judgment, however, the four issues just listed will prove crucial to the ultimate success of health care reform.

QUALITY ASSESSMENT AND IMPROVEMENT

A sound reform proposal should be able to assure the American people that control of the costs of health care is not being achieved through unintended reductions in the quality of those services. Many of the findings and recommendations in *Medicare: A Strategy for Quality Assurance* (IOM, 1990g) can be applied directly to a health care reform proposal that covers the entire population. We recommend that you include in your reform proposal the following three provisions concerning quality of care, which are derived from that report.

Your health care reform proposal should make quality of care an explicit objective, based on a comprehensive definition of quality. Quality assurance cannot be an afterthought in the design and implementation of health care reform. To make sure that quality assurance and improvement are integral parts of the reform effort, quality needs to be an explicit objective in the statutes that authorize reform and in the regulations that implement those statutes. Any statement of this objective needs to proceed from a comprehensive definition of quality, such as that from our 1990 report: "Quality of care is the degree to which health services for individuals and populations increase the likelihood of desired health outcomes and are consistent with current professional knowledge."

The main emphases in this definition—on individual patients and populations, on health outcomes broadly defined, and on professional responsibility—are significant and support a commitment to private care and personal choice. An explicit reform objective incorporating this definition will underscore that cost containment and extension of health insurance coverage are not the only measures of success in your program. Developing a quality assurance venture based on this definition will require:

- adopting a broad set of outcome measures, including health-related quality of life and patient satisfaction, as well as the more conventional measures such as mortality;

- giving specific attention to lack of necessary and appropriate services as well as to inappropriate use of services and poor technical or interpersonal care; and

- basing the program on the best scientific knowledge about outcomes and effectiveness and the links between processes and outcomes of care.

Consistent with that provision, your proposal should also adopt specific quality assurance goals. An effective reform program should be willing to be held accountable for:

- continuously improving the health of the population;

- enhancing the capabilities of health care organizations and clinicians of all kinds to improve performance for everyone, not just the "bad apples"; and

- identifying and overcoming system and policy barriers to improved performance.

These goals are consistent with the principles of continuous quality improvement and total quality management that have been successful in improving performance in the industrial and manufacturing sectors. In those arenas, applying these quality improvement techniques can lead to greater efficiencies in production and performance. Improving efficiency is, in our view, a significant step toward addressing the unfairness of our present health care system; making quality of care one of the core principles of your health care reform package thus promises to support the other critical aims of reform.

Achieving these goals will require an effective quality oversight and monitoring capability that is external to health care provider organizations; it will also call for better internal capacities for providers to continuously improve the quality of the care they render. The IOM report on Medicare quality assurance offers 15 attributes on which such efforts can be based and later judged, and the strategy for accomplishing all these ends applies directly to the broader environment of health care reform. It argues for:

- a strong emphasis on patient outcomes and individual well-being;

- appropriate measurement of the processes of care;

- consideration of the continuity of quality assessment across all settings in which health care is given, which we regard as particularly important when so many services are moving outside traditional institutional settings; and

- expanded efforts to collect, analyze, and feed back information on quality of care and performance to health care providers and consumers.

Finally, your reform plan should provide for investment in the research and data necessary for quality assurance. The above goals will not be attained unless support is given now to the development of essential knowledge and information about the effectiveness and appropriateness of health care *and* about the effectiveness of techniques to measure and improve quality. Although much has been learned about these issues in recent years, much more needs to be known and applied. Any commitment to quality of health care in a reform proposal implies a long-term effort to build the knowledge base and the capacity for quality assurance and improvement. Later in this paper we discuss steps that will be essential in developing and applying the knowledge necessary for a quality assurance approach that will monitor and guide health care toward desired outcomes.

VALUE IN HEALTH CARE

A principal objective of health care reform is to reduce the rate of increase in health care expenditures. Given the other objectives of reform, however, cost control can only be approached effectively from the perspective of value. What are we getting for our expenditures? Are we using resources efficiently and appropriately to achieve desired health outcomes, including preventive services? That we have only partial answers to these questions accentuates our concerns about the share of national resources devoted to health care. Several IOM reports suggest how we might obtain fuller information about the value achieved for different kinds of health care spending.

Your health care reform plan should provide adequate support for effectiveness and outcomes research. IOM committees have addressed the promises and limitations of research on effectiveness and outcomes in health care in a series of reports (IOM, 1989, 1990a,b,d,f). This work stresses the important distinction between effectiveness and efficacy. Efficacy is typically defined as the outcome of an intervention when it is applied in "ideal" circumstances, such as those in prospective randomized clinical trials. In contrast, effectiveness refers to the outcome of an intervention when applied in the daily practice of medicine to the medical problems of typical patients.

Among the key aspects of effectiveness research are generating accurate, valid, and reliable data; following patients over time and across settings of care; comparing alternative approaches to care; and tracking a broad range of patient-relevant outcomes including quality of life and health status as reported by patients. The creation of the medical effectiveness program of the Agency for Health Care Policy and Research (AHCPR), which was established in late 1989 in the U.S. Public Health Service, was an important step in expanding research on effectiveness and outcomes.

Effectiveness research complements the biomedical research that provides the scientific substrate of both clinical medicine and clinical epidemiology, which emphasizes the incidence and prevalence of disease. Effectiveness research adds an important dimension to these efforts by helping physicians, other health professionals, patients, the public, and policymakers better understand what can be expected from alternative courses of care, a key
requirement for making determinations about value. Adequate support of effectiveness research as well as biomedical research, therefore, is a necessary and integral part of any health care reform plan that hopes to improve the value received for our investments in health care.

Similarly, your plan should support the development and effective application of guidelines for clinical practice. The development and appropriate use of clinical practice guidelines helps us translate the knowledge gained from research into better health care. In *Clinical Practice Guidelines: Directions for a New Program,* and later in *Guidelines for Clinical Practice: From Development to Use*, IOM committees defined practice guidelines as "systematically developed statements to assist practitioners and patient decisions about appropriate health care for specific clinical circumstances" (IOM, 1990a, 1992c). The IOM has urged that such guidelines should describe the strength of the scientific evidence behind them and the outcomes and costs expected from their application.

Practice guidelines cannot be viewed as the solution to the health care cost problem. Systematically developed, science-based guidelines should, however, improve the quality of care (and its measurement) and help reduce the financial costs of inappropriate, unnecessary, or dangerous care. Practice guidelines, validated over time by outcome measures, are useful tools to improve the value in health care even when the result is additional, but appropriate, services.

In addition to its mandate to conduct effectiveness research, AHCPR is also promoting the development of practice guidelines, an effort that builds on and augments the work of many professional and research organizations that are committed to improved clinical practice. To advance these undertakings, the IOM's reports (IOM 1990c, 1992a) have defined the attributes of good guidelines; discussed their effective and appropriate application in quality assurance and improvement, cost management, and risk management and medical liability; and described a framework for improving the future development and use of guidelines.

We recommend that your health care reform proposal strongly endorse efforts to develop, apply, and evaluate practice guidelines and actively promote the effectiveness and biomedical research that builds the scientific base for guidelines. In your support for these endeavors you should adopt a long-term view, because sound programs to develop and apply authoritative guidelines are truly in an early stage of evolution. More directly, placing costs and cost containment strategies in the context of value, as well as building the quality assurance and improvement infrastructure, will require sustained support and commitment.

SPECIAL POPULATIONS: CHILDREN AND PREGNANT WOMEN

Universal access to health insurance, significant as it will be on ethical and practical grounds, does not equal access to health care. Thus, a thorough health care reform proposal must give attention to certain special groups (such as AIDS patients, the frail elderly, those with severe mental disorders, minorities, and the poor) to ensure that changes aimed at the broader population do not inadvertently leave segments of the population still facing difficult barriers to high, quality, affordable health care and improved health status.

For no group is this concern more acute than for children and pregnant women, especially those who are at high risk, either medically or socioeconomically. We recommend, therefore, that your reform package give specific attention to these parts of our nation's population in three major areas.

Your health care reform plan should include, as part of its package of benefits, those cost-effective services that are critical to the health and well-being of children and pregnant women. In *Including Children and Pregnant Women in Health Care Reform,* the IOM and National Research Council (NRC) (IOM/NRC, 1992b) assessed whether the current array of proposals for health care reform adequately addressed maternal and child health needs. The gaps in many plans were appreciable. As discussed in that report, meeting the health needs of this population means that the benefit package must cover critical and cost-effective services, including routine immunizations, well-child care, family planning services, dental care, and nutritional supports. Another recent IOM report (IOM, 1991b), *Disability in America: Toward a National Agenda for Prevention,* also makes similar points about prenatal diagnosis and care, family planning, maternity outreach, and related services for women in high-risk groups.

Even persons who do have insurance of some type (including Medicaid) may find that the health services they need are not those that are covered. Fewer than half of private insurance plans, for example, cover immunizations, and in an effort to control costs, some managed care plans now decline to pay for more than 24 hours of hospital care following normal childbirth, thus reducing the opportunity to monitor newborns in the critical first one or two days after birth and to teach new mothers how to care for their babies. These missing pieces of primary and preventive services ought, in our view, to be a fundamental part of your Administration's reform plan.

Adequate nutrition services are especially critical for this population. Your plan should make provision for the delivery of basic, patient-centered, individualized nutritional care as an integral part of primary care for every woman of child-bearing age and her infant, beginning before conception and extending throughout the period of breast feeding. The specific components of such care are described in two recent reports (IOM, 1992b; 1992c): *Nutrition During Pregnancy and Lactation* and *Nutrition Services in Perinatal Care.*

Your reform proposal should also support the training and deployment of the primary care personnel, as well as the operations of the health care systems, necessary to ensure access to essential maternal and child health services. Ample evidence exists that many areas of the country have too few primary care practitioners (doctors, nurses, dentists, and other health professionals providing primary care) and health clinics, that the nation's medical schools and graduate training programs continue to produce more specialists than primary care physicians, and that we train far too few mid-level practitioners such as certified nurse-midwives. We would note that changing the emphasis in the U.S. health system towards primary care is important for the population as a whole, not just for mothers and children. In 1978, an IOM report noted the decline in the number of primary care practitioners available to provide adequate primary care to the entire population and recommended that at least 50 percent of physicians be trained as primary care practitioners. (IOM, 1978). We would emphasize that, in addition to training more primary care practitioners, the conditions and rewards of practice need to be changed to make career pathways in primary care more attractive.

The support of public sector networks, such as special grant programs that provide children and pregnant women with health and social services, is essential to ensure access to necessary services for this population. Strong evidence also exists that, especially for low-income, high-risk children and families, care offered through comprehensive community-based centers, involving a team of health professionals, is more effective than the care provided through private physicians, because the needs of the population are often greater than a single office-based practice can accommodate.

Accordingly, we recommend that your Administration's proposal for health care reform support the existing network of comprehensive services for children and pregnant women. Such systems need to be reviewed, strengthened, and increased in underserved communities; a review of European networks of special centers for children, pregnant women, and families may have great relevance to reform ideas for the United States.

Your reform plan should provide for effective mechanisms of administration, cost management, and quality assurance that take the needs of children and pregnant women directly into account. This population is not well equipped, as a general proposition, to cope with complicated administrative structures that cut across the public and the private sectors. Furthermore, the challenges of utilization management requirements, as well as the often formidable financial barriers posed by cost-sharing requirements, may prove significant obstacles to obtaining appropriate, effective, and timely maternal and child health services. A vigorous, well-financed system of quality assurance and an energetic program of health services research will help protect against some of these problems, as discussed earlier in this report. In addition, we advise that your plan acknowledge all these special concerns about children and pregnant women so that other potential oversights or even threats to their well-being as reform moves ahead can be successfully averted. A particular issue is that, for this population, care outside of hospitals and nonmedical factors, such as food supplements, is particularly important, and measures of utilization and outcomes may be more difficult.

Investment in health services for mothers and children will pay dividends for society, not only in savings of future health care costs, as documented in our reports, but in broader social and economic benefits as well. We commend your prior commitment to this objective as shown by your actions as Governor.

HEALTH CARE DATA AND INFORMATION

Successful health care reform will require more and better data and information about health care, especially if the health care system is under stress as it tries to hold down expenditures while expanding access and maintaining high-quality care. Such a circumstance will require an improved ability on the part of health care providers, patients, the public, and policymakers to make informed choices and trade-offs.

Previous sections of this paper have already indicated the need for improved data and information for operations, evaluation, and research. A comprehensive quality assurance system will require a greatly enhanced data base on use of services, patient outcomes, and the process of care. The creation of that data base, only the foundations of which currently exist, will be a major undertaking that will take a number of years to implement fully. This makes more important the commitment we believe your reform proposal needs to make to the development and implementation of a firm plan for a data base for quality monitoring and improvement.

Your health care reform plan should support development and universal adoption of a computer-based patient record. In a recent report, *The Computer-based Patient Record: An Essential Technology for Health Care*, an IOM committee explored the problems of today's patient records, which are still predominantly paper based, and the opportunities afforded by a shift to computer-based systems (IOM, 1991a). Universal adoption of a computer-based record promises all the following: (1) better patient information to support clinical decisions; (2) improved management of care by making quality assurance procedures and clinical practice guidelines more accessible to health care professionals at the time and site of patient care; (3) reduced administrative costs; and (4) more relevant, accurate data necessary for provider and consumer education, technology assessment, health services research, and related work concerning the appropriateness, effectiveness, and outcomes of care.

Complete development and adoption of a computer-based record will be a lengthy and challenging task. Initial steps have been taken to implement the detailed strategy set out in the IOM report; these include creation of a computer-based patient record institute and research on topics such as privacy and confidentiality of health records. Stating in your health care reform proposal a commitment to move toward computer-based patient record systems will provide a further impetus to complete this technological and behavioral revolution, and it will underscore the importance your Administration might place on information and electronic technologies as a bedrock of progress on controlling costs, expanding access, and improving quality.

Your plan should commit your Administration to use specific outcome and utilization indicators to monitor access to personal health services. In the debate about health care reform, lack of health insurance coverage is often equated with lack of access. In fact, insurance coverage, although a factor that clearly influences access to care, is actually a rather crude and imprecise proxy for access to and use of needed and appropriate services. Until recently experts have not agreed on a set of more meaningful indicators of access. In *Access to Health Care in America* (1993), the IOM offers a set of reliable and valid indicators that will map directly to comprehensive health reform efforts. These indicators include access-sensitive outcomes (levels of screening for treatable diseases such as breast and cervical cancer) and measures of utilization of health services (e.g.,rates of persons with acute illness who have no physician contact in a year) that are known to be linked to desired patient outcomes; all can be derived from existing data sources.

If these indicators are tracked over time, then the nation will have a much better gauge of the effects of policies and programs intended to improve access. Because guaranteed universal coverage is a core principle of your reform plan, it seems to us imperative that your Administration put in place a means of monitoring progress and identifying other barriers to access that are not removed by extending health insurance coverage. This may be especially critical for certain special populations, such as children and pregnant women. The IOM's access indicators will be crucial evaluation tools for health care reform, and efforts should be made now, through survey techniques and other means, to establish the baselines against which progress and failure can be measured over time.

Your reform plan should also provide for a national health care survey that can track progress and identify problems in the implementation of your Administration's reform efforts. From the time of the first national census in 1790, an important role of the federal government has been to provide objective statistical information to inform and guide the individual decisions and social policies of a free society. The National Center for Health Statistics (NCHS) has long carried out important parts of this federal role in the health field, especially with regard to vital statistics and national survey data about health status and utilization of health services.

In light of the rapid changes in health care and the prospect of further changes, the NCHS has proposed an innovative national health care survey intended to greatly improve our knowledge about the functioning of the health care system. A joint IOM/NRC committee, in *Toward a National Health Care Survey: A Data System for the 21st Century* (IOM/NRC, 1992a). has made suggestions for this survey to ensure that it will be an even better source of data about the use and effects of health services. These national data would complement information derived from health care operations, such as insurance claims forms and computer-based patient records. Knowledge derived from the survey and the resulting database would also create new opportunities to understand patterns of care, costs of care, health status and other characteristics of individuals receiving care, and their demand for and use of services over time and across a broad range of providers and service settings. The improved information will help improve professional performance and equip consumers to make better choices about health care.

By providing objective data, consistent over time and across the country, the NCHS survey would provide an important evaluation tool for health care reform. We regard its early development and implementation by your Administration as a critical component of an effective, long-term reform strategy.

CONCLUSION

Your commitment to significant health care reform is clear and widely welcomed. We expect that specific details of your plan will focus initially on universal access and cost containment. The purpose of our suggestions and recommendations in this paper is to underscore the importance of other key elements of reform, without which, in our view, even the most well-conceived and well-implemented reform efforts may not realize their full potential. In our judgment, your Administration's plan should address quality assessment and improvement, the value of health care, special populations (especially children and pregnant women), and health care data and information. The IOM stands ready to assist you and your Administration in a comprehensive effort to improve the health and well-being of the American people through major health care reform during your first term of office.

REFERENCES

IOM. 1978. *A Manpower Policy for Primary Care.* Washington, D.C.: National Academy Press.

IOM. 1988. *The Future of Public Health.* Washington, D.C.: National Academy Press.

IOM. 1989. *Effectiveness Initiative: Setting Priorities for Clinical Conditions.* Washington, D.C.: National Academy Press.

IOM. 1990a. *Acute Myocardial Infarction: Setting Priorities for Effectiveness Research.* P. Mattingly and K.N. Lohr, editors. Washington, D.C.: National Academy Press.

IOM. 1990b. *Breast Cancer: Setting Priorities for Effectiveness Research.* K.N. Lohr, editor. Washington, D.C.: National Academy Press.

IOM. 1990c. *Clinical Practice Guidelines: Directions for a New Program.* M.J. Field and K.N. Lohr, editors. Washington, D.C.: National Academy Press.

IOM. 1990d. *Effectiveness and Outcomes in Health Care. Proceedings of a Conference.* K.A. Heithoff and K.N. Lohr, editors. Washington, D.C.: National Academy Press.

IOM. 1990e. *Healthy People 2000. Citizens Chart the Course.* M.A. Stoto, R. Behrens, and C. Rosemont, editors. Washington, D.C.: National Academy Press.

IOM. 1990f. *Hip Fracture: Setting Priorities for Effectiveness Research.* K.A. Heithoff and K.N. Lohr, editors. Washington, D.C.: National Academy Press.

IOM. 1990g. *Medicare: A Strategy for Quality Assurance.* Vols. 1 and 2. K.N. Lohr, editor. Washington, D.C.: National Academy Press.

IOM. 1991a. *The Computer-Based Patient Record: An Essential Technology for Health Care.* R. Dick and E.B. Steen, editors. Washington, D.C.: National Academy Press.

IOM. 1991b. *Disability in America. Toward a National Agenda for Prevention.* A.M. Pope and A.R. Tarlov, editors. Washington, D.C.: National Academy Press.

IOM. 1992a. *Guidelines for Clinical Practice: From Development to Use.* M.J. Field and K.N. Lohr, editors. Washington, D.C.: National Academy Press.

IOM. 1992b. *Nutrition During Pregnancy and Lactation. An Implementation Guide.* Washington, D.C.: National Academy Press.

IOM. 1992c. *Nutrition Services in Perinatal Care.* Second Edition. Washington, D.C.: National Academy Press.

IOM/NRC. 1992a. *Including Children and Pregnant Women in Health Care Reform.* Summary of Two Workshops. S.S. Brown, editor. Washington, D.C.: National Academy Press.

IOM/NRC. 1992b. *Toward a National Health Care Survey: A Data System for the 21st Century.* G.S. Wunderlich, editor. Washington, D.C.: National Academy Press.

IOM. 1993. *Access to Health Care in America.* M.A. Millman, editor. Washington, D.C.: National Academy Press.

V

SUMMARIES OF SELECTED RECENT REPORTS OF THE NATIONAL RESEARCH COUNCIL

NATIONAL ACADEMY OF SCIENCES
NATIONAL ACADEMY OF ENGINEERING
INSTITUTE OF MEDICINE
NATIONAL RESEARCH COUNCIL

Summaries of Selected Recent Reports
of the National Research Council

As part of the information made available by the Academy complex for the incoming Clinton administration, the presidents of the National Academy of Sciences, the National Academy of Engineering, and the Institute of Medicine authorized the preparation of brief summaries of ten, potentially high impact reports issued during the previous 18-24 months by various committees of the National Research Council (NRC), which they jointly manage. The summaries, which are representative of the more than 200 reports produced annually by the NRC, were selected on the basis of (a) their relevance to current national policy concerns, (b) the extent to which their major conclusions and recommendations remain unimplemented, and (c) the extent to which they represented the major program elements of the institution. In all, ten summaries are presented, representing the work of eight program units of the NRC. At the end of each summary, the name of the relevant contact person is provided, along with the full title of the report summarized.

IMPROVING AMERICA'S DIET AND HEALTH

Food and Nutrition Board
Institute of Medicine

People can reduce the risk of several chronic diseases by their choice of foods. This fact has been disseminated widely and most Americans are aware of it. By the late 1980s a majority of Americans surveyed knew that a high-fat diet increases the risk of heart disease. Fewer people, but still a sizable proportion of the population, also knew that dietary fat is a risk factor for high blood pressure and cancer and that salty foods are related to hypertension.

Many people are trying to change their eating patterns, but there is such an array of processed foods available, it is not easy to know how well one is eating. Consumption surveys reveal considerable confusion. While people are eating more vegetables, fruits, and grains--a healthy sign--they also are consuming more high-fat cheeses, rich ice creams, snack foods, candy, beer, and wine. In other words, just telling people they should change their diets to improve their health and leaving the rest up to them isn't enough. There must be a better balance between individual and societal responsibilities. This means that society as a whole-- government at different levels, the food industry, restaurants and supermarkets, health care professionals, educators, and the media--should be involved in helping consumers choose healthier foods.

About five years ago, the federal government and several private organizations issued recommendations based on what is known about the relationship of diet and various diseases. Subsequently, the U.S. Department of Agriculture and other federal agencies adopted a Food Pyramid, the new good guide that embodies these recommendations, replacing the Basic Four.

Where does the country go from here? As policymakers study ways to contain health care costs, it becomes apparent that preventing disease and promoting good health makes sound economic sense. It follows then that encouraging dietary changes and making it easier for Americans to eat a diet that reduces the risk of chronic diseases fits into the nation's health care needs.

A concerted effort, not unlike the broad program mounted to convince Americans to stop smoking or not to start smoking, is needed. Although smoking, as an addictive habit, is very different from eating, the campaign to change eating habits also must be waged on several fronts. Antismoking efforts extend to restrictions in public buildings and work places; examples of nonsmoking by famous people; education by school teachers, health providers, and the media; and programs to help people stop smoking. A similar societywide effort would go a long way toward changing eating patterns.

Each in its own way, the various sectors of society need to initiate approaches based on three strategies: creating an atmosphere supportive of dietary change; altering the food supply to facilitate new eating patterns; and providing people with practical, useable information about how to improve their diets.

Federal, state, and local governments should implement the dietary recommendations in a consistent manner throughout all government enterprises. At the federal level both the Department of Agriculture and the Department of Health and Human Services have programs to promote their dietary recommendations, and other federal agencies participate in interagency nutrition activities, but many knowledgeable observers describe federal efforts as fragmented and falling short of the goal. Establishment of a coordinating mechanism would provide greater direction to governmentwide efforts.

The dietary recommendations should be implemented in programs related in some way to food, from education to health care to farm policies to research support. Promoting these goals may require some congressional action. For example, the last Congress contributed to dietary improvements when it passed a law requiring that food labels be redesigned to make them easier to understand and better focused on the nutrients of greatest concern. Government also should foster programs and practices that will disseminate nutrition information to the public and encourage food suppliers to increase the availability of healthful foods. It is particularly important that the principle of dietary guidelines be followed in restaurants, hospitals, and other places where individual diners have no control over the nutritional content of the food they eat. Price supports, food safety, food stamps, school lunches, agricultural trade--all are government programs that directly or indirectly affect the diets of Americans.

Governments and health care professions must become more active as policymakers, role models, and agenda setters. For government this means that public feeding programs should follow the dietary recommendations. This would include assistance programs for low-income families as well as government food services such as Army messes, employee cafeterias, and veterans' hospitals. Government cafeterias that offer healthful choices would serve as models to the public.

All sectors of society will not agree with these efforts. Although the food industry has taken the initiative in making low-fat, low-salt, sugarless, and other healthful foods available, it and other interest groups are likely to object to policies they perceive will place them at a competitive disadvantage. Change will come incrementally as individuals and food suppliers gradually accept and adapt to the new goals. The time frame will be years or decades--not weeks or months.

The task is large, but doable, if everyone in a position to influence public behavior joins the effort.

For more information: *Improving America's Diet and Health*, National Academy Press, Washington, D.C., 1991

Contact: Paul Thomas, Institute of Medicine, (202) 334-2587

NUCLEAR POWER:
TECHNICAL AND INSTITUTIONAL OPTIONS FOR THE FUTURE

Energy Engineering Board
Commission on Engineering and Technical Systems

Over the last four decades, nuclear energy has become the second largest source of electricity in America, behind only coal. America's 111 commercial power plants provided about 20 percent of the country's electricity in 1990. In several other countries, the percentage of electricity generated by nuclear energy is even higher: 77 percent in France, 33 percent in West Germany, and 26 percent in Japan.

However, the expansion of nuclear energy has virtually halted in the United States. No new nuclear plant has been ordered in the United States since 1978, scores of plants ordered earlier have been canceled, and construction of at least seven partially completed plants has been deferred.

A number of factors account for nuclear power's stagnation. These include reduced demand for electricity, high costs of nuclear power, regulatory uncertainty, and public concern over safety and over waste disposal issues.

The risk to public health from the operation of current reactors in the United States is very small. In this fundamental sense, these reactors are safe. A significant segment of the public has a different perception, however, believing that the level of safety of nuclear power plants can and should be increased.

In 1988 the Senate Appropriations Committee asked the National Academy of Sciences to analyze the technical and institutional alternatives that would preserve the nuclear fission option in the United States. This request was based on the premise that nuclear fission will remain an important alternative for meeting U.S. electric energy requirements and maintaining a balanced national energy policy.

The study's purpose was not to advocate a new generation of nuclear power plants or to assess the desirability of nuclear power relative to alternative energy sources. Instead, the study committee, consisting of members with a wide range of views on the desirability of nuclear power, approached its charge with the intent of determining <u>what would be necessary if the United States is to retain this option to meet electric energy requirements in the future.</u>

If nuclear power is to be retained as a viable option for the United States, a number of institutional and technical changes will be necessary:

● To make the costs of nuclear power competitive with other sources of electricity and to assure the recovery of capital and operating costs, the industry must develop better methods for managing the design and construction of nuclear plants.

● Participants in the design and construction of nuclear plants must institute arrangements that guarantee timely, economical, and high-quality construction of new plants. Such arrangements will be prerequisites for receiving assurance from state regulatory authorities, in advance of construction, that capital costs can be recovered. Financial backers and electricity generators must be satisfied of such arrangements before new plants can be ordered.

● Plant designs that are more nearly complete before construction begins and plants that are easier to construct will provide greater confidence that costs can be controlled. Better construction and management methods and business arrangements that provide strong incentives for cost-effective, timely completion of projects will also contribute to greater confidence. Utilities, architect-engineers, and suppliers of nuclear technology should begin now to work out such arrangements.

● A consistently higher level of demonstrated utility management practices in some operating plants in the United States is essential before the public's attitude about nuclear power is likely to improve. Over the past decade, utilities have strengthened their ability to be responsible for the safety of their plants. The nuclear industry should continue to take the initiative to bring the standards of every American nuclear plant up to those of the best plants in the United States and the world. Chronic poor performers should be identified publicly and should face the threat of insurance cancellation.

● To retain nuclear power as an option, a high degree of standardization will be very important. A strong and sustained commitment by the nuclear industry will be required to realize the potential benefits of standardization.

● Lack of resolution of the high-level nuclear waste problem jeopardizes future nuclear power development. The legal status of the Yucca Mountain storage site should be resolved soon; investigations of this site should continue. A contingency plan to store high-level waste in surface storage facilities pending the availability of the geologic repository must be developed.

● The EPA standard for disposal of high-level waste has to be reevaluated to ensure that the standard applied to the geologic waste repository is both adequate and feasible.

The committee offered several recommendations for institutional change, including:

● The Nuclear Regulatory Commission should develop a coherent, consistent set of regulations for advanced reactors, especially light water reactors with passive safety features.

● The Nuclear Regulatory Commission should encourage industry self-improvement, accountability, and self-regulation initiatives.

● The industry and state should cooperate closely to ensure that state economic incentives and state oversight of safety remain consistent with safe operation of nuclear plants.

● A small safety review entity, analogous to the National Transportation Safety Board, should be established to investigate serious nuclear accidents. Before such an entity is established, its charter, reporting channels, and the classes of accidents it would investigate should be carefully defined.

The committee also assessed the prospects for a number of advanced reactors now in development. It considered safety, economic, technological, and institutional factors in its assessments. The committee concluded that large light water reactor designs (about 1,300 megawatts), now evolving from existing reactor designs, and mid-sized light water reactors (about 600 megawatts) with passive safety features, now in design stages, best satisfied the committee's criteria. The large reactors are likely to be ready for construction first, by about the year 2000. The mid-sized reactors will be ready soon after 2000. These two reactors should be safer than existing reactors if design goals are realized. Little or no federal funds are necessary to complete development of the evolutionary reactors, though such funding would accelerate the process. Federal funding will be necessary for the development of the mid-sized reactors.

In considering the long term, the committee concluded that liquid metal reactor technology, which would yield reactors capable of breeding plutonium for nuclear fuel and thus extending nuclear fuel resources, could be an important long-term technology and should have highest priority for long-term nuclear technology development.

The committee analyzed three alternative research and development programs. Each contained common elements, including support for improved performance and life-extension of existing reactors, support for university research, and money for certain nuclear facilities. The three alternatives were differentiated by the extent of support for the development of specific reactor technologies. The committee judged that an alternative should be followed that would add to the common elements support for mid-sized light water reactor development and support for liquid metal reactor technologies. This alternative could permit construction of liquid metal reactors in the second quarter of the next century.

For more information: *Nuclear Power: Technical and Institutional Options for the Future,* National Academy Press, Washington, D.C., 1992

Contact: Dev Mani, National Research Council, (202) 334-3344

AUTOMOTIVE FUEL ECONOMY:
HOW FAR SHOULD WE GO?

Energy Engineering Board
Commission on Engineering and Technical Systems

Automobiles and light trucks consume almost 60 percent of the petroleum used in the United States, which is somewhat more than the total amount of petroleum that this country imports. Following the oil embargo of 1973, the U.S. Congress acted to limit the country's vulnerability to oil supply interruptions by passing the Energy Policy and Conservation Act of 1975. This act required that each manufacturer's domestically produced and imported fleets of new cars meet a "corporate average fuel economy," or CAFE, standard of 27.5 miles per gallon (mpg) by 1985, a standard that has stayed the same since then. For light trucks, the corresponding standard is now 20.4 mpg. Although a number of other factors also played roles, this law contributed to almost a doubling of fuel efficiency for the U.S. new car fleet over the last 17 years.

Over the last several years a contentious debate has flared over whether these CAFE standards should be increased. On one side are those who argue that we should require vehicles to achieve better gas mileage so as to limit the United States' dependence on imported oil and reduce carbon dioxide emissions. On the other side are those who say that boosting CAFE standards will increase traffic fatalities, raise the price of new vehicles, reduce sales, and seriously harm the automobile industry.

The intensity of this debate heightened in the fall of 1991 when the Persian Gulf conflict began. At that time the federal government asked the National Research Council to study the prospects for further improving the fuel economy of light-duty vehicles. The 16-member Committee on Fuel Economy of Automobiles and Light Trucks concluded that it is indeed technically possible for all classes of new cars and trucks to have significantly higher levels of fuel economy by the year 2006 while complying with the Clean Air Act Amendments of 1990 and existing and pending standards for occupant safety. Using currently available technologies and maintaining current vehicle characteristics valued by consumers, fuel economy levels could rise to between 34 and 37 mpg by that year for new cars and to between 26 to 28 mpg for light trucks, assuming that the future mix of vehicles remains the same as today.

But there is a difference between what is technically possible and what is practically achievable. Complex tradeoffs need to be made between the benefits of higher fuel economy standards and such costs as the following:

- Increasing fuel economy levels by that amount will add between $500 and $2,750 to the average price of a new vehicle. Furthermore, the provisions of the Clean Air Act Amendments of 1990 and current and pending safety regulations will further boost the costs of new light-duty vehicles.
- If manufacturers increase fuel economy by reducing the size and weight of cars and light trucks, safety could be somewhat reduced, though improved vehicle design and safety technology could offset effects of weight reduction.
- Stricter tailpipe emissions standards that are expected in future years could make it harder to achieve increased fuel economy, since they may increase the weight of the car or rule out emerging fuel-saving technologies.
- And the automobile industry, on the heels of an unprecedented downturn that has resulted in hardship for many workers, is ill-prepared to make additional investments required by new fuel economy demands.

The practically achievable fuel economy level for new cars in the year 2006 is likely to be somewhere between the 34-37 mpg that is technically achievable and the 27.8 mpg that prevails today. However, many past predictions of automotive fuel economy have erred badly, and unexpected new technologies may boost efficiencies appreciably. By the same token, average fuel economies have fallen for the last four years as consumers have opted for heavier and higher performing cars, and fuel economy could stagnate if current trends and policies remain unchanged.

Any government action to boost fuel economy levels should include a hard look at the current CAFE system, which has serious defects. As gasoline prices have dropped in real terms over recent years, the CAFE standards have increasingly conflicted with market signals. They have also disadvantaged manufacturers that make both large cars and small cars (including the American manufacturers) compared to manufacturers that specialize in small cars (including the Japanese manufacturers). Furthermore, the distinction between domestic and foreign fleets has distorted the way manufacturers allocate production of vehicles to their U.S. and foreign facilities. In addition, U.S. companies, unlike their foreign competitors, may face charges of unlawful conduct if they violate CAFE standards and choose to pay penalties for noncompliance.

A number of more flexible alternatives or supplements to the CAFE system need to be considered, including:

- increased gasoline prices, which would affect the use of all cars on the road and not just the characteristics of new cars;
- a system of cash fees and rebates (known as "feebates") for inefficient and efficient vehicles to increase consumer interest in improved fuel economy;
- strategies to trim the number of vehicle miles driven, new inspection programs, and methods of trapping gasoline vapors to reduce emissions; and

- improving the transportation infrastructure, developing intelligent vehicle-highway systems, improving public transit, reducing speed limits, and encouraging car-pooling.

All of these options need to be carefully investigated to help foster a transportation system that can readily adapt to new circumstances.

For more information: *Automotive Fuel Economy: How Far Should We Go?* National Academy Press, Washington, D.C., 1992

Contact: Mahadevan (Dev) Mani, National Research Council, (202) 334-3344

NEW APPROACHES TO REDUCING OZONE POLLUTION

Board on Environmental Studies and Toxicology
Commission on Geosciences, Environment, and Resources
Commission on Life Sciences

Despite public and private expenditures of billions of dollars on pollution controls, many American cities and suburbs are still plagued by high levels of ozone. A major component of smog, ozone near the ground can cause reduced lung capacity and other harmful effects in humans and can damage vegetation. The Environmental Protection Agency reported that in 1989 over a quarter of all Americans lived in areas where ozone levels exceeded the National Ambient Air Quality Standards (NAAQS) established through the Clean Air Act amendments of 1970. Ozone pollution remains a serious health and environmental concern.

Ozone near the ground forms when nitric oxide (NO) and nitrogen dioxide (NO_2), together referred to as NO_x, react with volatile organic compounds, or VOCs, in the presence of sunlight. (Ozone high in the atmosphere, in contrast, which shields the ground from harmful ultraviolet radiation emitted by the sun, forms through a different chemical process.) NO_x enters the atmosphere from the combustion of fossil fuels, primarily in motor vehicles, electricity power plants, and other large industrial facilities. VOCs also come from motor vehicles; in addition, they are given off by the chemical and petroleum industries, by evaporating paints and solvents, and by vegetation.

The Clean Air Act requires that the states design and implement strategies that will bring each area exceeded the NAAQS into compliance. These strategies are known as State Implementation Plans, or SIPs. In principle, they are a sound way of reducing ozone levels. But, according to the National Research Council's Committee on Tropospheric Ozone Formation and Measurement, they have failed in practice, largely because they have relied on estimated inventories of the amount of ozone precursors released into the atmosphere rather than on actual atmospheric measurements of those precursors.

The problem is that these inventories are often in error. For example, the inventories have significantly underestimated the release of VOCs from human activities. As a result, the substantial reductions in ozone concentrations expected to follow reductions in VOCs emissions have often not occurred.

Existing flaws in today's ozone control system point toward major new directions for future efforts. First, the underestimation of VOCs in emissions inventories implies that many ozone control strategies have been misdirected. These strategies have usually focused on reducing VOCs, but given their high levels it makes more sense, in many cases, to concentrate on reducing NO_x in addition to or instead of reducing VOCs. For example, in many parts of the eastern United States the level of VOCs from vegetation alone, when combined with existing levels of NO_x, is enough to raise ozone levels to the unhealthy range on hot summer days. However, in some areas, such as the centers of large cities, reducing NO_x may actually increase ozone, though ozone levels would likely decrease downwind.

In general, the concentrations of ozone precursors need to be much more carefully monitored to verify the effectiveness of emissions controls. New instruments are being developed to measure these precursors more reliably; this work should continue, and the new techniques should be applied much more widely.

A related problem is that the computer models used to understand and predict ozone levels are still subject to many uncertainties. These models need to be studied and improved. Better models will help determine the most effective way to reduce ozone in a given area. Intensive field programs will be needed to evaluate, improve, and verify the models.

Another important application for these models is assessing the effects of alternative fuels --including natural gas, methanol, ethanol, hydrogen, and electricity--on ozone levels. Today, not enough is known to require the widespread use of any specific fuel to reduce ozone levels (with the possible exception of electricity, which would shift emissions from mobile sources to fixed power plants). Better models would help specify where alternative fuels can make a major difference.

Finally, the principal measure used to track ozone trends needs to be supplemented or replaced by measures that are more statistically valid. The measure specified by the NAAQS (the second highest concentration each year in a one-hour period) is highly sensitive to the vagaries of weather and is not a reliable indictor of progress in reducing ozone over several years in a given area. In fact, it is often difficult, using the specified measure, to tell if ozone exposures are going up, going down, or staying the same. New measures need to account for the effects of weather and other relevant factors and should reflect the range of ozone concentrations considered harmful to human health and welfare.

Many of these recommended actions would benefit substantially from a national program of research on ozone near the ground similar to the program that has been developed for ozone high in the atmosphere. Properly insulated from regulatory and political pressures, a broadly based but carefully coordinated research program would help establish a reliable scientific basis for improving the nation's air quality.

For more information: *Rethinking the Ozone Problem in Urban and Regional Air Pollution,* National Academy Press, Washington, D.C., 1992

Contact: Raymond Wassel, National Research Council, (202) 334-2617

<u>Report Summary</u>

HIGH SPEED TRAINS

Transportation Research Board

In Europe and Japan many trains travel at speeds approaching 200 miles an hour. The Japanese "bullet train" regularly reaches 163 mph, while the French Train à Grande Vitesse Atlantique is capable of 186 mph peak performance. In contrast, the fastest train in the United States is the Amtrak Metroliner between Washington, D.C., and New York City, which operates at a top speed of 125 mph.

The question repeatedly asked by members of Congress and other policy makers, along with returning American tourists: Why doesn't the United States have high-speed trains?

Since World War II the U.S. public has relied almost exclusively on personal automobiles for relatively short trips and commercial airlines for more distant journeys. Except for a few busy corridors--the Washington-Philadelphia-New York-Boston route, for example--trains in the United States mostly carry freight, not people.

This situation has been perpetuated in part by the way government regulation and funding institutions have been organized around specific modes of transportation rather than around a national transportation system. Roads and airports have been routinely supported by taxes and user fees designated for that purpose, while railroads have not received the same level of aid. Europe and Japan, on the other hand, have a long tradition of publicly supported national railroads.

Many U.S. highways and air transport facilities currently are strained to capacity, and travel demand is expected to continue to increase. Construction of new highways and airports, however, has been stymied by right-of-way restrictions; public opposition to the air pollution, noise, and other environmental disruptions that accompany major building projects; and high costs.

As alternatives, high-speed rail and magnetic levitation ("maglev") systems are often proposed. High-speed rail includes both upgraded existing lines as well as completely new systems operating on dedicated tracks with lightweight trains and fully automated signals and communications. Maglev systems featuring vehicles that are suspended above a fixed guideway by powerful magnets appear to be a promising technology for the future. However, development is still in the early stages and substantial additional research is needed. In short test runs, maglev vehicles have attained speeds of 270 to 320 mph.

In the short term, greater speeds could be attained by upgrading existing rail systems through such changes as realigned tracks, gas turbine-powered trains, modern signalling systems, and improved grade crossings. Amtrak Metroliner service between Washington and New York recently announced introduction of a Swedish "tilt" train that can take curves at higher speeds without jarring passengers and thus can travel about 25 mph faster.

But achieving speeds higher than 150 mph will require systems with new, exclusive-use guideways, and such high speed rail and maglev systems do not come cheaply. Estimates for newly constructed systems in the United States have run from $8 million to $32 million per mile for fast trains and $11 million to $63 million per mile for maglev. Cost estimates are extremely uncertain, however, because a high-speed rail or maglev system has never been built in the United States. Cost varies with the technology, site characteristics, and land values.

It is highly unlikely that farebox revenues alone could pay the bill for construction and operation of a new high-speed rail or maglev system. For the most likely combination of cost and fare levels, the break-even passenger volume would be roughly 6 million annual riders. Air traffic, which would be the primary market for new systems in most corridors, currently exceeds this level for only one city-pair combination. In the Northeast corridor, where there is significant rail ridership today and a rail line can serve multiple cities, the prospects for break-even operation would be good if right-of-way could be found and capital costs kept below $18 million per mile.

Public subsidies for new construction and upgrading could be justified if improvements in rail service can attract passengers away from overcrowded highways and airports and can delay or avoid new investments in these modes. In selected areas--the Los Angeles-San Francisco corridor, for example--fast rail service might avoid the need for a new airport and free up much needed gate capacity in existing airports. In such cases existing transportation funds could appropriately be tapped to subsidize the new rail services. Other anticipated benefits of high speed rail include the use of less energy per passenger mile and stimulation of economic development around intercity terminals.

The U.S. Department of Transportation and state transportation agencies should evaluate rail systems in the context of alternative airports and highway investments to determine the most cost-effective approach to improving intercity travel. This will require new approaches to planning that move away from a focus on specific modes of transportation to consideration of a national transportation system.

If a decision is made to implement high-speed rail, the technology must be imported because there are no current U.S. manufacturing capabilities. European and Japanese manufacturers can provide off-the-shelf high-speed rail technology that has been proven in commercial service. However, these systems, while achieving good safety and operating records, do not meet current U.S. rail safety standards. As assessments of costs and benefits for potential high-speed corridors are taking place, federal regulators should continue development of appropriate safety and operational standards.   Then if decisions are made to build new high-speed rail systems and conduct further research on maglev, the necessary regulations and standards would be in place.

For more information: *In Pursuit of Speed: New Options for Intercity Passenger Transport,* Transportation Research Board, Washington, D.C., 1991.

Contact: Walter J. Diewald, Transportation Research Board, (202) 334-3255

DOMESTIC AIR TRANSPORT SINCE DEREGULATION

Transportation Research Board

The deregulation of the airline industry in 1978 was, on balance, a good thing. It has resulted in better passenger service, lower average fares, and no measurable loss of safety. The industry has become more efficient and competitive. However, some troublesome signs have appeared that could threaten the benefits achieved.

The airline industry has always been highly sensitive to economic cycles, but the sharp decline in international air travel during the Gulf War and a protracted recession have caused massive losses. The precarious financial condition of several carriers raises concern that the number of major carriers could be reduced below the level needed to provide adequate competition. Although the current down-cycle has reduced peak-period demands placed on airports and the air traffic control system, capacity limitations will be encountered again once demand for air travel resumes its historic growth rate. Institutional constraints on the performance of the Federal Aviation Administration (FAA) raise doubts about its ability to meet future challenges posed by continued air transport growth.

Deregulation diminished government control of prices and entry of new airlines into the commercial market, but it did not remove government oversight of air traffic control, carrier maintenance inspections, and other safety measures. The FAA continues to be responsible in these areas. This entails maintaining a highly skilled staff of controllers, maintenance technicians, safety inspectors, engineers, and test pilots -- a force that was seriously dissipated in the last decade by a series of problems starting with the firing of most senior air traffic controllers during a labor dispute in 1981. In recent years, the FAA has worked diligently to rebuild its specialized staffs, but has been further hampered by delays in the delivery of highly sophisticated, new traffic control equipment and software, government hiring ceilings, and tight budgets.

Despite labor shortages, FAA has maintained a high level of safety. However, to ensure safe travel, air traffic controllers frequently impose considerable delays on departure of commercial flights, particularly during inclement weather. As the number of airline passengers continues to grow in the future, delays can be expected to increase. The aging of commercial aircraft also will demand greater vigilance from FAA maintenance inspectors. Future safety could be endangered if carriers cut back on maintenance practices because of economic pressures or the FAA's inspection service is hampered by funding and staffing difficulties.

The FAA would be better positioned to meet future demands if it can surmount certain constraints characteristic of a government agency. These include not only hiring, procurement, and funding limitations, but also the disruptions caused by frequent turnover of administrators. A stable, long-term leadership is required for the kinds of system-wide reforms that would enable the FAA to fulfill its complex, high-technology mission more effectively.

Three options for institutional change have been proposed: re-establishment of the FAA as an independent federal agency outside the Department of Transportation (DOT); a government corporation; or a private corporation.

The first option, while giving FAA more freedom in management, would not remove other government constraints and therefore would not provide the flexibility needed. Under the framework of a public or private corporation, either the entire FAA or only its air traffic control component could be transferred from the DOT. As a public corporation, the FAA would report either to the President and Congress or to the DOT Secretary. Operation as a congressionally chartered private corporation could embrace only the air traffic control operations or Congress could, by law, imbed within the corporation a legally independent government unit to oversee the broad range of safety standards and practices.

Either a public or private corporation would improve the efficiency of the air traffic control service and offer more managerial discretion in funding, personnel, and procurement; a private corporation obviously would provide the greatest flexibility. Some observers argue that it would compromise safety to separate the traffic control service from the rest of FAA.

Before Congress takes any action, it should mandate a study by an independent organization of the possible reform scenarios for FAA and their probable outcomes.

Another area of possible concern is the recent concentration of the domestic airline industry to a few carriers. Despite the initial flurry of new entries following deregulation, mergers and acquisitions diminished the number of carriers. Originally some airlines took this course as a means of expanding routes. More recently, however, economic problems have forced a number of airlines to merge or cease operations. Eastern, Pan American, and Midway all ceased operating in 1991. America West, Continental, and Trans World are reorganizing under Chapter 11 bankruptcy procedures. An infusion of foreign capital into struggling carriers such as Northwest and USAir has prompted a fractious debate on the appropriateness of foreign entry into the domestic market.

In its 1991 report, the Transportation Research Board of the National Academy of Sciences addressed the effects of mergers and acquisitions of domestic carriers on competition. It concluded that the Department of Justice, acting under antitrust authority, should oppose a merger when it would reduce the number of competitors offering parallel service or sharing a hub airport. Mergers of airlines offering complementary or "end-to-end" routes, however, may not harm competition. The largest benefits to the traveler occur in markets with three or more carriers. To assure this level of competition would require five or six firms engaged in nationwide competition, with at least three competing at most large airports.

Although the Academy report did not consider the costs or benefits of foreign entry, the recommendation that an adequate level of competition should be retained to protect consumers against price gouging would be a major component in the decisions concerning investments in U.S. carriers by foreign carriers, as well as in mergers between two domestic lines.

For more information: *Winds of Change: Domestic Air Transport Since Deregulation*, National Academy Press, Washington, D.C. 1991.

Contact: Stephen R. Godwin, Transportation Research Board, (202) 334-3255

Report Summary

DISPOSING OF HIGH-LEVEL RADIOACTIVE WASTE:
A NEW APPROACH

Board on Radioactive Waste Management
Commission on Geosciences, Environment, and Resources

In the Nuclear Waste Policy Act of 1982, Congress set in motion a process to dispose of the tons of spent nuclear fuel that have been filling the storage pools at U.S. nuclear power plants. It gave the Department of Energy (DOE) responsibility for designing and eventually operating a deep geological repository for high-level radioactive waste. It required that the Nuclear Regulatory Commission license the facility when construction is completed, and it directed that releases of radionuclides from the facility result in no more than 1,000 deaths over a period of 10,000 years as specified in a standard established by the Environmental Protection Agency.

Most high-level waste comes from the 111 nuclear power plants now operating in the United States. The typical large power plant generates about 30 tons of spent fuel a year, most of which is currently cooling in rapidly filling storage pools at each reactor site.

There is worldwide scientific consensus that the best way to dispose of this waste is to bury it deep underground. There is no scientific or technical reason to think that a satisfactory geological repository cannot be built.

But the U.S. program, as conceived and implemented over the past decade, is unlikely to succeed. The program assumes that the properties and future behavior of a geological repository can be determined and specified with great certainty for thousands of years into the future.

But this degree of certainty is unattainable. Geological environments are never completely predictable, which will inevitably require that the program be modified as it progresses. Scientific analysis can and should play a key role in assessing long-term geological repositories. But preparing quantitative predictions so far into the future stretches the limits of our understanding of geology, groundwater chemistry and movement, and the interactions between emplaced materials and their surroundings.

These technical problems are exacerbated by a series of highly charged political realities. People feel threatened by radioactive waste, and their views deserve to be taken seriously in the decision-making process. To negotiate equitable solutions, technical experts and program managers need to provide the public with information that the public finds believable. The government must also recognize that public participation, negotiation, persuasion, and compensation need to be fundamental parts of a waste management program.

Instead of pursuing the elusive goal of scientific certainty, an alternative approach should be pursued, similar to the approaches now being followed in Canada and Sweden. Three principles should guide this effort:

- Start with the simplest description of what is known, so that the largest and most significant uncertainties can be identified early in the program and given priority attention.
- Meet problems as they emerge, instead of tying to anticipate in advance all the complexities of a natural geological environment.
- Define the problem broadly in terms of ultimate performance rather than in terms of immediate requirements, so that increased knowledge can be incorporated in the design at a specific site.

This alternative uses modeling as a tool to identify areas where more information is needed rather than to justify decisions that have already been made on the basis of limited knowledge. Implicit in this approach is the need to revise the program schedule, the repository schedule, and performance criteria as more information is obtained. Putting such an approach into effect would require major changes in the way Congress, the regulatory agencies, and DOE conduct their business.

Uncertainty does not necessarily mean that the risks of a geological repository are significant. A successful management plan can accommodate these uncertainties and still provide reasonable assurance of safety. The public can be assured that the likelihood of serious unforeseen events (serious enough to cause catastrophic failure in the long term) is minimal, but these assurances will rely on general principles rather than detailed predictions.

In the final analysis, safety is in part a social judgment, not just a technical one. How safe is safe enough? Moreover, is it safer to leave the waste where it is, mostly at reactor sites, or to put it in an underground repository? In either case, safety cannot be 100 percent guaranteed. Technical analysis can help answer such questions, but ultimately the answers depend on choices made by the citizens of a democratic society.

In summary, DOE's high-level waste program may be a "scientific trap" for DOE and the U.S. public alike, encouraging the public to expect absolute certainty about the safety of the repository for 10,000 years and encouraging DOE program managers to pretend that they can provide it.

For more information: *Rethinking High-Level Radioactive Waste Disposal: A Position Statement by the Board on Radioactive Waste Management,* National Academy Press, Washington, D.C., 1990

Contact: Peter Myers, National Research Council, 334-3066

Report Summary

U.S. EXPORT CONTROLS
IN THE POST-COLD WAR ENVIRONMENT

Committee on Science, Engineering, and Public Policy

Rapidly occurring events during the past few years have fundamentally changed the nature and sources of the threats to U.S. national security. The dissolution of the Soviet Union and the overthrow of communist governments among its Eastern European allies in the Warsaw Treaty Organization have brought an end to the immediate threat of aggression in Western Europe. But the dramatic changes have not produced a world free of international tensions. In place of a clearly defined, monolithic threat, the United States now must be prepared to counter a variety of military and economic challenges.

Militarily, the threat now comes largely from countries that have acquired -- or are attempting to acquire--the means to produce and deliver nuclear, chemical, and/or biological weapons, which are often referred to as weapons of mass destruction (WMD). A country that attains this capacity may use its new strength to agitate long-standing regional rivalries through acts of terrorism or even open aggression, as Iraq did in 1990. There is evidence that, at present, India, Israel, Iraq, Pakistan, and South Africa may possess or be close to possessing nuclear weapons. Only Iraq is known to have used chemical weapons in recent warfare, but more than 12 nations outside of NATO and the Warsaw Pact are now believed to have them.

Economically, the threat to U.S. stability comes from many directions. Japan and the European Community are the major competitors for international trade, but newly industrialized countries such as Korea, Taiwan, and Brazil also are making inroads on traditional U.S. markets. Analysts and policymakers acknowledge that U.S. national security now includes maintaining a successful, vigorous role in the global economy.

For more than 40 years, the United States and its allies cooperated to prevent the Soviet bloc from acquiring advanced technologies for military purposes. Export controls regulated sales of weapons and also of "dual use" technologies, which are those items useful in civilian as well as military enterprises. Since 1949, the task of coordinating the West's restrictions on export of sensitive items has been carried out by the Coordinating Committee for Multilateral Export Controls (CoCom), an informal, non-treaty organization consisting of all members of the North Atlantic Treaty Organization (except Iceland), plus Japan and Australia.

In the new global environment, the export controls that served well during the Cold War no longer meet U.S. needs. They have not prevented proliferation of weapons of mass destruction to nations involved in regional conflicts, and they may be obstructing U.S. industries in their quest to remain competitive in world markets. The old system should be reformed and redirected in response to today's new proliferation challenges.

In relations with the former Soviet Union, the U.S. government and CoCom can now move safely from a policy of general denial of dual-use technologies to a policy of presumed approval to export, with the approval dependent on the ability to verify that dual-use products actually are being used for civilian purposes. Verification is feasible in the new, more open environment of the former Soviet Union. But export controls cannot yet be discarded altogether. Although the former Soviet Union no longer appears either inclined or capable of mounting a conventional attack against the West, it remains the only country in the world with enough nuclear weapons to destroy the United States and the other CoCom countries. A delicate balance must be drawn between the need to relax restrictions sufficiently to promote economic reconstruction and the shift to a market-based economy, while also maintaining vigilance against the possibility of a major political reversal and attendant change in Russian foreign policy.

At the same time, a much higher priority now must be placed on controlling proliferation of WMD and missile delivery systems to states believed to be arming for the purpose of engaging in regional aggression. Such developments constitute a national security concern for the United States and should be given major emphasis. Working in concert with other nations, including the former Soviet Union and China in addition to U.S. allies, the United States should strive to minimize proliferation of arms to countries considered threats to the peace. Cocom, working with other international regimes, may be a possible mechanism for developing export controls designed specifically for this purpose. (Since the National Academy of Sciences report was released, a "CoCom Cooperation Forum" has been established in the former Soviet bloc specifically to address proliferation concerns. The Forum involves virtually all of the republics of the former Soviet Union as well as the East European countries that previously were members of the Warsaw Treaty Organization.)

Meanwhile, meeting economic challenges will require changes in the domestic management of export controls. Following the premise that government should present as simple a face as possible to those being governed and regulated, the federal government should adopt a more flexible and responsive trade policy. The new approach should include simpler licensing procedures and easier understood regulations for American manufacturers competing for world markets. In the past, unilateral controls, most of them related to U.S. foreign policy concerns, often prevented U.S. industry from selling products that foreign competitors were free to sell on the open market. The complexity of the U.S. export control system led some American companies to give up attempts at international trade entirely and some foreign manufacturers to avoid buying U.S.-made components.

The President should issue a national security directive that clearly states the objectives of all national security export controls, including controls on munitions; dual-use products; missiles; and technologies related to the development of nuclear, chemical, and biological weapons. This directive would establish criteria and mechanisms for constructing control lists that balance military, economic, and foreign policy factors and detail the process for resolving disputes between agencies.

The administration of export controls should be consolidated under the U.S. Commerce Department's Bureau of Export Administration, but policy should continue to be made by the three agencies traditionally involved: the Departments of State, Defense, and Commerce. An Export Control Policy Coordinating Committee, composed of senior representatives from relevant departments and agencies, should be created to formulate and review export control policies and resolve difficult disputes. An industry advisory committee also should be established and required by law. Furthermore, laws prohibiting industry from seeking judicial redress for export administration decisions should be repealed.

The world is changing in many ways. As economic power replaces military prowess as the touchstone of global leadership, the United States must adapt its policies to the new realities.

For more information: *Finding Common Ground: U.S. Export Controls in a Changed Global Environment*, National Academy Press, Washington, D.C., 1991.

Contact: Mitchel B. Wallerstein, National Research Council, (202) 334-2168

Report Summary

U.S. TRADE IN THE WORLD ECONOMY

Committee on National Statistics
Commission on Behavioral and Social Sciences and Education

The U.S. economy is becoming increasingly internationalized. This may not sound like anything new because people have been buying French wine and Japanese cars for years. The trade imbalance with imports outstripping exports year after year has been going on for some time, and the figures are dutifully reported to the public and periodically lamented by commentators.

But far more is occurring in the global marketplace than a simple exchange of goods and services between countries. U.S. statistics [adjusted for inflation] show that over the decade of the 1980s, while U.S. gross national product rose 30 percent, U.S. imports and exports of goods and services increased 72 percent. During the same period, foreign direct investment in U.S. real estate, businesses and industries, and related assets tripled in value, and similar U.S. direct investment abroad increased by 60 percent. Meanwhile, the total value of purchases and sales between U.S. and foreign residents in U.S. and foreign long-term securities increased almost 20 times. The U.S. economy is considerably more interdependent with those of other countries than ever before.

Yet, the data collection system for U.S. international transactions was developed for a simpler era. Although efforts have been made from time to time to improve the data, major shortcomings remain. Today, multinational companies may have roots in one country, but their affiliates span the globe and buy and sell abroad. Advanced telecommunications transfer capital instantaneously, making international banking activities, exchanges of securities, and other investment transactions possible without going through domestic financial intermediaries. As a result, significant portions of U.S. international business activities are not covered in the existing data.

The fast-paced global economy offers a myriad of challenges and opportunities for the United States.   To deal effectively with the challenges and take full advantage of the opportunities, both public and private sectors need timely, accurate, and relevant information on burgeoning U.S. international economic activities.

U.S. trade performance is now charted largely by what is called the balance-of-payments system, which tracks the movement of goods, services, and capital across national boundaries. A system based simply on cross-border transactions is inadequate for analyzing new economic issues arising from the emerging international economic order. For example, it does not capture the sales and purchases of goods and services by foreign affiliates of U.S. firms abroad and U.S. affiliates of foreign firms in the United States. Those transactions are several times larger than the combined value of U.S. imports and exports.

The federal government should develop a "supplemental framework" for measuring U.S. international business performance that tracks both cross-border transactions and business activities undertaken by foreign affiliates of U.S. firms abroad and U.S. affiliates of foreign firms in the United States. Such a framework would offer a clearer look at the nation's international competitiveness. It would also provide insight into how jobs are gained or lost in the United States because of foreign investment here and U.S. investment abroad.

A study panel of the National Research Council recently examined data collected on international transactions in goods, services, and capital flows. On the basis of its estimates, U.S. businesses could well be competing more vigorously in the world economy than widely publicized trade statistics suggest.

For example, the government reported that in 1987 the U.S. trade deficit in goods and services was $148 billion. Using the proposed supplemental framework, the panel estimated that there were $1,303 billion in U.S. purchases from foreigners and $1,239 billion in U.S. sales to foreigners in 1987, leaving a $64 billion difference. This paints a much different picture of U.S. international performance than that portrayed by the U.S. trade balance figure, in which $484 billion in imports of goods and services was subtracted from $336 billion in exports for a deficit of $148 billion. The study panel used 1987 data because they were the most recent available when the study began.

The published trade numbers don't tell the whole story, and at times they tell the wrong story about the U.S. trade position. Several other important developments are obscured in the current data. One is the increasing trade between corporations and their own foreign affiliates. In 1987, for example, more than a quarter of the reported U.S. imports and exports was the result of such intracompany activities. Intracompany trade covers a variety of transactions, including situations in which a corporation manufactures its components in one country and ships them to an overseas affiliate for assembly. A related development is the fact that products are no longer simply "Made in the U.S.A." or "Made in Taiwan." Many imported and exported goods, such as automobiles and computers, contain components from many countries.

Even services can involve·a multinational effort. Companies from different countries can collaborate on projects ranging from computer software development to advertising campaigns.

Trade statistics suffer, as well, from a dearth of information on international services transactions, such as international financial services and tourism, and sizable flows of capital in and out of the country. These capital flows include securities transactions in which U.S. residents can legally buy and sell directly in overseas markets without going through U.S. financial institutions that are required to report such transactions. Better information on capital flows is needed for a number of purposes, including assessing the impact of foreign direct investment on the domestic economy, measuring the extent of the credit crunch, and monitoring the safety and soundness of the U.S. financial system.

The accuracy, coverage, and usefulness of information on U.S. international transactions can be enhanced through stricter enforcement of reporting requirements and automated data collection procedures. Information from airport audits, comparisons of U.S. merchandise export figures with corresponding foreign import figures, and statistical analyses suggest that the value of U.S. merchandise exports to major trading partners has been underreported by 3 percent to 7 percent. This could mean that exports are being underreported by $10 billion to $20 billion, and the trade deficit overstated by 20 to 30 percent, based on 1991 estimates of merchandise exports.

Data collection agencies should work closely with users of the data to ensure that relevant statistics are being collected for intended uses. Stronger ties to firms that file the data also would ensure greater compliance and cooperation, which would enhance the accuracy of the data.

For more information: *Behind the Numbers: U.S. Trade in the World Economy,* National Academy Press, Washington, D.C., 1992

Contact: Anne Y. Kester, National Research Council, (202) 334-3290

UNDERSTANDING AND PREVENTING VIOLENCE

Division on Social and Economic Studies
Commission on Behavioral and Social Sciences and Education

In cities, suburban areas, and even small towns, Americans are fearful and concerned that violence has permeated the fabric and degraded the quality of their lives. The diminished quality of life ranges from an inability to sit on the front porch in neighborhoods where gang warfare has made gunfire a common event to the installation of elaborate security systems in suburban homes where back doors once were left open. Children in urban schools experience violence on the way to school and in the school building itself. Surveys show that large percentages of the population fear even walking in their neighborhoods at night. The nation's anxiety on the subject of violence is not unfounded.

There is substantially more violent crime reported in the United States than in almost any other developed country. Homicide rates far exceed those in any other industrialized nation. For other violent crimes, rates in the United States are among the world's highest and substantially exceed rates in Canada. In 1990 alone, violent crimes resulted in the death of more than 23,000 Americans.

The number of violent crimes has remained constant at about 2.9 million per year. Injury occurs in only about one-third of them, and the victim is killed in fewer than four of every 1,000 violent crimes. Even when death or injury is avoided, losses to victims and society are sizable.

Who commits violent crimes? Offenders are overwhelmingly male (89% of those arrested) and are disproportionately drawn from racial and ethnic minorities. Men in the 25-29 age range are more likely than any other group to commit violent crimes. One quarter of nonfatal violent crimes are committed by multiple offenders.

Society has responded to increasing rates of violence by lengthening prison sentences. The average time served for a violent crime nearly tripled between 1975 and 1989. Although estimates of the effects of incarceration are imprecise, longer prison stays have not reduced violent crime.

In considering crime control policies and legislation, analyses suggest that further lengthening of time in prison would have a very small effect. However, increasing the <u>certainty</u> of going to jail does appear to have an effect. It has been estimated that a 50 percent increase in the probability of incarceration would prevent twice as much violent crime as a 50 percent increase in the average term served. Achieving such an increase in certainty, however, would require substantial improvement in crime reporting and greater investments in police investigation and prosecution.

This analysis suggests that preventive strategies may be as important as criminal justice responses to violence. The success of preventive strategies depends on understanding more about the roots of violence. How does a potential for violence develop in individuals? What circumstances are conducive to violent events? What social processes foster violence?

Policy makers and researchers should test and evaluate additional strategies for controlling violence. Just as the causes of violence are complex, no single approach will succeed in controlling all types of violence. One promising area of study would attempt to identify factors that influence an individual's potential for violent behavior. For example, aggressive children may grow into aggressive adults, but most of them do not. The distinguishing factors may be related to socioeconomic status. Identifying the relevant characteristics of communities, families, and persons should be of the highest priority in future research. Certain characteristics of low-income communities, for example, may promote violent behavior in some children.

An approach to understanding prevention and control of violence--a perspective with roots in both criminology and public health--is to focus on the places where violence occurs. A great deal is known about how the configuration of public spaces either facilitates or discourages violence, but this knowledge is not widely used. For example, public housing developments in communities occupied largely by broken families and unsupervised adolescent children of working single parents are high-crime areas. Several public housing developments have been designed to provide greater safety from violence, and experience with these projects is providing useful information about the safe management of public spaces in high risk areas.

There also should be studies to measure the effectiveness of police activities in reducing violence associated with illegal markets, particularly in drugs.

Deaths from guns are high in the United States compared with other countries and are rising, especially among young black males. More than 80% of the firearms used in violent crimes are reportedly obtained by theft or through illegal or unregulated transactions. Therefore, while pubic debate continues over new firearms legislation, much could be accomplished as well by evaluating how better to enforce existing laws governing the purchase, ownership, and use of firearms. Strategies might include disrupting illegal gun markets by police use of many of the same tactics currently used for dispersing illegal drug markets, enforcing existing bans on juvenile possession of handguns, and neighborhood-oriented police work involving close coordination with community residents.

Searching for possible physiological processes that underlie violent acts is another area of study that needs to be explored. The psychosocial development of an individual who engages in violent behavior is potentially influenced by genetics, neurobiologic characteristics, and consumption of alcohol and other psychoactive drugs. Research should be conducted to find new pharmaceuticals to reduce violent behavior without debilitating side effects.

Emerging patterns and problems of violence are sometimes slow to be discovered because the systems for gathering information have not been fully developed. A high priority should be placed on modifying and expanding computer databases to provide more detailed information about the extent, causes, and possible control of violent behavior.

Federal support for research into violence and its prevention and control should be increased to learn more about the physiological, emotional, and socioeconomic factors behind violent responses by individuals. This should include funding assistance to states and localities for experimentation in new approaches to dealing with violence.

For more information: *Understanding and Preventing Violence*, National Academy Press, Washington, D.C., 1992

Contact: Susanne A. Stoiber, National Research Council, (202) 334-3730

9252